FUNKY
BUSINESS
FOREVER

FT Prentice Hall
FINANCIAL TIMES

In an increasingly competitive world, we believe it's
quality of thinking that gives an edge – an idea that opens
new doors, a technique that solves a problem, or an insight
that simply helps make sense of it all. The more you
know, the smarter and faster you can go.

That's why we work with the best minds in
business and finance to bring cutting-edge thinking
and best learning practice to a global market.

Under a range of leading imprints, including
Financial Times Prentice Hall, we create world-class
print publications and electronic products bringing our readers
knowledge, skills and understanding, which can then be
applied whether studying or at work.

To find out more about Pearson Education publications, or tell
us about the books you'd like to find, you can visit us at
www.pearsoned.co.uk

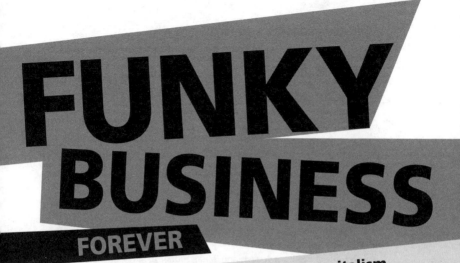

FUNKY BUSINESS

BUSINESS

FOREVER

How to enjoy capitalism

Jonas Ridderstråle & Kjell Nordström

 Prentice Hall
FINANCIAL TIMES

An imprint of **Pearson Education**
Harlow, England • London • New York • Boston • San Francisco • Toronto
Sydney • Tokyo • Singapore • Hong Kong • Seoul • Taipei • New Delhi
Cape Town • Madrid • Mexico City • Amsterdam • Munich • Paris • Milan

PEARSON EDUCATION LIMITED

Edinburgh Gate
Harlow CM20 2JE
Tel: +44 (0)1279 623623
Fax: +44 (0)1279 431059

Website: www.pearsoned.co.uk

First published in Great Britain in 2000
Second edition published in 2002
Third edition published in 2008

© BookHouse Publishing AB, Stockholm, Sweden 2002, 2008

The right of Kjell Nordström and Jonas Ridderstråle to be identified as authors of this work has been asserted by them in accordance with the Copyright, Designs and Patents Act 1988.

This edition is not for sale in the United States, Sweden, Norway, Denmark and Finland.

ISBN: 978-0-273-71413-2

British Library Cataloguing in Publication Data
A catalogue record for this book is available from the British Library

10 9 8 7 6 5
12

Typeset in 9.5/14pt DIN Regular by 30
Printed and bound in Great Britain by Clays Ltd, Bungay, Suffolk

The publisher's policy is to use paper manufactured from sustainable forests.

CONTENTS

FEELING FUNKY 206

INTRODUCTION

Built to blast

It was love at first sight. When we came up with the title *Funky Business* we knew we were on to something. It nailed down what we had been talking about for a few years in a neat and memorable slogan. And it worked. People understood the meaning of funky business. Some, unfortunately, did so without reading the book. Other people in more than 50 countries throughout the world plucked up courage, removed a book written by two shaven-headed Swedish academics from the bulging business bookshelves and bought a copy. The result is that *Funky Business* has now been translated into more than 30 languages – three more languages than our combined doctoral dissertations sold copies.

A few things you should know about *Funky Business Forever*: seeking inspiration our first port of call was all the people who had registered an interest in our work at our website. We asked them about their worlds. What were the things that had changed over the past few years? What was going to change in the future? How did they feel? What did they fear, what turned them on? Thousands of emails flooded in. We would like to thank each and every person who found the time to make contact. We have listened – though we haven't necessarily always agreed!

We have also tried to make this a much leaner publication. As a result, some of our more esoteric and academic references have been eliminated. If you want to chase up a particular reference for the sake of completeness please send an email to info@funkybusiness.com.

Ideas are a debate. Always. So, if you have further thoughts, gripes and insights about anything contained within these

pages please make contact directly with us –
funksters@funkybusiness.com.

Of course, the world in which *Funky Business* appeared in
2000 was a radically different one from the one we can now
see outside the frosted corporate windows. In 2000 the dot-
com frenzy was at its height – and the Spice Girls were still
together. Al Gore was a slightly dull safe-pair-of-hands vice
president, rather than a charismatic environmental
campaigner. Enthusiasm and entrepreneurial vigour, tinged
with the usual capitalistic cocktail of avarice and partially
clothed ambition, filled the air. Then dot-com stocks hit the
buffers, 9/11 took our breath away and the world became a
harsher, more questioning, place. Yet, since then the market
has made a remarkable comeback, and the BRIC economies –
Brazil, Russia, India and China – and others have expanded at
astonishing rates.

Funky Business struck a chord. The book – to our minds at
least – was never simply a dot-com-new-economy-funkfest.
The ideas in *Funky Business* had germinated over a lengthy
period and have carried on germinating and developing – most
obviously in our next book, *Karaoke Capitalism.* The
phenomena we talked about in *Funky Business* were
highlighted under the media spotlight of the new economy, but
they were virtually always long-term trends in the way we
manage organisations, the aspirations of individuals, the role
of society and so on. The funky economy was not the new
economy of *Wired* or *Fast Company* circa 1999. Instead, it was a
global change in the way people think and behave: *built to blast*
rather than *built to last*. This was and is a book about what is
new in our economy, rather than the *new economy*.

The other thing which *Funky Business* was decidedly *not* was
a how-to book. We observed a profusion of trends and
happenings. We gathered together bits of data and wild and
wacky happenings from strange and amusing places. We put
many of these on Post-it notes and decorated a room with
them. This upset our Swedish passion for sensible
minimalism. We wanted to make sense of what we saw. And

that is what the book set out to do. *Funky Business* made sense of the world as we saw it. It does not tell you what to do tomorrow. Why should it? How could it? Instead, *Funky Business* encourages people to start taking notes on what they see and feel in their personal and professional lives. Seeing and believing is the root of action. There is nothing so funkily practical as a great idea.

As well as being filed under 'new economy' and suspicions about the practicality of our ideas, some readers of *Funky Business* expressed surprise that the book was written by two Swedish academics. Indeed, some people did not read the book precisely for that reason. To them, we apologise. But, try as we might, we have failed to transform ourselves into straight-down-the-middle, plain-vanilla academic types. There are also some good reasons why *Funky Business* was written by Swedes. Sweden in general, and perhaps Stockholm in particular, embraces modernness with unique lustful vigour. The underlying big idea which has driven Sweden over the past few decades has been the intent to destroy the manuscript of the past – deregulating life by giving people – particularly women – the freedom to know, go and do whatever they wanted, regardless of gender, social class, or any other traditional inhibition.

This brought great emphasis on education and personal freedom, but also a lack of stability. This has made young Swedes experienced in surviving and thriving under conditions of high uncertainty. For better and worse, we are unfamiliar with the concept of lifelong loyalty – to a country, company, partner, husband or wife – because we have never experienced it. Sweden was preparing for our uncertain times even when it had no idea they were destined to be uncertain.

About this book

That's it: no more explanations and excuses. *Funky Business* isn't a practical, new-economy book written by b-school profs from the mid-West. It is resolutely and unashamedly funky.

And so to business: *Funky Business Forever* is a unique idea. Normally, when authors revisit past glories they write a quick introduction to provide a certain distance and then leave the main text gloriously untouched, like an artefact in a literary museum. We admit that this crossed our minds. But then we started re-reading *Funky Business*. This was an odd experience, like bumping into an old friend in a bar and discovering that you still have a lot in common though your stomachs might have grown, your hair disappeared, and your tastes changed.

As we read the book, there were things we disagreed with. Sometimes we turned out to be less brilliantly prescient than we had imagined. China, we lament, is largely notable for its absence. Sometimes the examples had dated. We still loved *Funky Business*, but thought we could do more than simply endorsing another edition with a new cover.

Funky Business Forever is the result. What we have done is to look at *Funky Business* through the lens of the latter part of the millennium's first decade. We have cut a number of examples, updated figures where necessary and provided a running commentary where our thinking has evolved – or been evolved for us. We also asked thousands of readers for their thoughts on the past few years and what they see unfolding in the years to come. Many thanks to all who took the time to connect with us and our ideas.

We hope the end result is as timeless as it is determinedly funky: *Funky Business Forever.*

The heat is on

Let's re-funk: How has the world changed since 1999?

Well, the first thing to note is that it has changed a great deal. Change is a fact of life. Tourists and refugees inhabit our world, says Italian artist Francesco Clemente – either you embrace change or you try to escape from it. The problem for the latter group is that in an increasingly transparent and globally connected world, Motown's Martha and the Vandellas were indeed right. There is nowhere to run, and nowhere to hide.

The big issue just got bigger. If you had to select one key issue on the world's agenda it must be climate change. Climate is no more and no less than the temperature in Fahrenheit or Celsius. Hurricanes, polar ice caps melting, tsunamis and so on are simply the effects of this. No business book can solve climate change, but a book can make a difference in shaping organisations and leaders who consider broader responsibilities than the balance sheet.

The trouble is that this has become increasingly difficult. There is something very similar to climate in our economic and social systems: the amount of information we pump out to our fellow human beings. In personal and organisational terms this can be as noxious as CO_2 emissions to the climate. Look around and think back. We have changed the climate in our societies beyond comprehension. And when we change the social and economic climate every human activity is affected – in politics, business, spirituality, education and beyond.

Sceptical? Well, look back at recent history. The Soviet Union fell because Moscow could not control the flow of information in and out of the country. The profusion of information meant that even the mighty Soviet system could no longer control its people. The transparency that follows from information being symmetrically and internationally distributed is extremely bad news for any dictator trying to bully citizens, customers or colleagues. Turn on Google Earth and take a tour of the democracies of the world. Think back to how many democracies existed 60 years ago.

The climate change also makes life more difficult for anyone, inside and outside organisations, who does not add value. Markets are simply big conversations where sellers and buyers exchange information to determine the price of something. They feed and breed on information. So, expect more markets and fewer hierarchies. Already, we are witnessing this in the financial services industry with the resurgence of private equity. The information jungle is less forgiving than the information desert.

From value to values. On Planet Transparency, the ground is covered with snow. You leave tracks. We leave tracks. Even William Jefferson Clinton left tracks. Behaviour, good and bad, is exposed. Corporate climate change can be seen in economic scandals such as at Parmalat, Worldcom and Enron. Does their spectacular and criminal folly suggest that there are more criminals in the information-rich world? No. But there is a changed climate. In an information-laden transparent society you do not get away with it. Good news.

Amid this info-mire, there are success stories aplenty. Low-cost solutions love climate change.

And what's the driving force? In *Funky Business* we argue that a potent combo of technology, institutions and values is the driver behind change. But, technology is now *the* key driver. Politics always beats business but technology always beats politics.

Technology opens up more markets and more things than ever before to total transparency and increased globalisation. As entry barriers come down, overcapacity becomes the norm. Simultaneously, the search costs for finding the best deal are rapidly decreasing and the Internet also provides a platform that enables customers to use their collective bargaining power. In effect, power is transferred from those who sell to those who buy. Forget about kings and queens. The new customer is a demanding dictator. The stupid, humble, loyal customer is a thing of the past.

Freedom rules. We have deregulated life and business life. Welcome to a world ruled by markets and man.

Funky truths for the noughties and beyond

That's the big picture – climate change and corporate climate changes driven by information and technology. A level below there are a host of Post-it notes now adorning our minds, random but decidedly funky scribblings on the phenomena of today and tomorrow:

#1: The tsunami of cheap

It is the age of cheap! A wave of cheapness in all industries except raw materials is breaking over western economies. It is only the beginning; 3.2 billion people – China + India + Russia + Brazil = BRIC – are on the move, industrialising their countries and absorbing knowledge with incredible speed. The BRIC phenomenon is no longer a distant dream.

Think: What do you plan to do when your market is flooded with cheap imports?

An interesting side issue to this is that we are seeing larger markets for both luxury and low-cost products. Wal-Mart is extremely good news for Gucci. What happened to all the talk of piracy killing luxury markets? Not true. Pirates and originals thrive, side by side. Julio de Castro of Spain's Instituto de Empresa business school has carried out research into this. He writes: 'Let's start in Beijing and its Silk Street Market, which is, in essence, a five-floor mall. A resident of China or a tourist can find here a profusion of luxury goods. Or, to be more precise, the consumer will find a profusion of products masquerading as luxury goods. On any given day, name brands will *appear* to beckon you to buy quality and buy cheap; from Rolex to Armani by way of Gucci and Burberry, the pirates seem to offer the impossible: high quality and low price. On the surface this seems like a simple story: those who pirate products are stealing profits from brand names. True, but five minutes away is a store that sells *real* Tag Heuer watches as well as other genuine watch models. The lesson is clear but counter-intuitive: piracy and legitimate brands can live side by side. Is there a new global truth emerging here?' De Castro thinks so and so do we.

#2: The age of women

We are seeing the feminisation of all human activity. EVEolution, a word coined by Faith Popcorn, is transforming women into an economic and executive force to be reckoned with. Visit Las Vegas and you will see that even the high temple of kitsch consumerism is bowing in the face of feminine power.

It is awash with spas and pamper parlours to lure women, as traditional gambling (men gathered round a table with smoke rising) is on the decline. From politics to business, religion to sport, women are in the ascendancy. Why? Now, we work with brains not brawn. Economic well-being depends on utilising everyone in society. Accept no excuses.

#3: Hit singles

Look around. Who are your neighbours? Increasingly they will be single households. Approaching 50 per cent of households in most major Western cities are people who, for one reason or another, live by themselves. In Stockholm 64 per cent of households are relishing their singledom. In London the figure is 42 per cent. This is only the beginning. Societies are being redefined as the legal, social, moral and domestic unit of analysis changes. Debenhams' store in Stockholm had special evenings for singles shopping – first you buy pickles and then make a pick-up.

#4: A world of cities

Nation states are neat arrangements when it comes to staging the Olympic Games or the World Cup, but they are no longer useful as economic measures. Instead, look at the world's cities. Increasingly, they are beginning to resemble the nation states of four or five hundred years ago. Instead of Genoa circa 1600 think Dalian, China; instead of Venice think Mumbai, India. Cities, not nations, are on the move. In less than 20 years more than 60 per cent of the world's population will live in cities. Where do you need to live?

#5: Fun filled

Welcome to the age of entertainment. As we write, Carsten Höller has masterminded an exhibition at London's Tate Modern gallery involving long, looping play slides in the gallery's foyer. Fun brings a premium price. To everything – whether it be museums, flying, or driving – entertainment is an increasingly essential add-on. There is fun in functionality –

The Unilever Series: Carsten Höller, Tate Modern Museum, London 2006 because it sells. The other thing to factor in is that fun is not something you do after you leave work. People want to play at work rather than play work. Look at the continuing success of Virgin, a company founded on fun and finance, and the global sweep of the iPod.

#6: Generic competition
You used to know who your enemies were. Competition used to be specific. Now it is generic. Now, we compete for money from banks, investors and customers rather than competing against companies with similar products and services.

#7: America über alles
The United States is still standing. Despite its economy losing its aura of invincibility with the emergence of India and China, the dot-com bust and the war on terror, the United States remains the economic powerhouse of the world. Why? Because of innovation. Why? Because innovation creates temporary monopolies which allow you to print money.

Why are Americans so innovative and, as a result, stinkingly affluent?

The answer is straightforward, dauntingly so. America's success lies in its ability to mop up the greatest talent. The brightest minds from China, India, Russia, Brazil and elsewhere flock to the US. Why? Because the US is an *idea* not a country. Anyone can become American. It doesn't matter whether they are Russian hockey players or Polish topless models. Give it two to four years and you become a full member of the movement. Try the same elsewhere and it takes a whole lot longer and involves a great deal more confusion. It takes two or three generations to become German, Spanish, Swedish or French. If you can't attract the best people, how are you going to create the world's most innovative place?

#8: Tacit knowledge rules
To survive and thrive you need to arm yourself with the most lethal of weapons: knowledge. What has happened since *Funky*

Business appeared is that knowledge has become even more vital. Articulated knowledge of any kind does not provide competitive advantage; but tacit knowledge does. Thankfully, we know more than we can say. Think of the corporate implications. Instead of organising along silos of functional knowledge, organisations will divide themselves according to the knowledge, aspirations and biographies of their people.

#9: The next level of work specialisation

Companies used to create and exploit. No longer. Look around and you will see that the acts of creation and exploitation are increasingly separated. On the one hand are companies geared towards exploitation – for example large multinationals – and on the other there are creation houses, smaller research-driven firms. This means that large companies will spend less time trying to turn themselves into funky design studios and more time working *with* funky design studios. Working with others is one of the great corporate challenges of the next decade.

#10: Capitalists anonymous

With our pensions and stocks in privatised companies and so on, we are all capitalists now. Look behind a big company name and you will now find another big institutional name. Look behind that and you will find another institution, and another. There are no owners in the conventional sense. Big capitalism is increasingly anonymous. Soon, there will be meetings at which attendees will begin by admitting: 'My name is John. I am a capitalist.'

#11: Interactive everything

Communication and pleasure used to be linear and discrete. Writing and reading. Foreplay and sex. Now, activities are entwined and interlinked in a bewildering array of combinations. The new logic is interactivity in everything. Welcome to the age of the combo where the mayo is mixing with the mustard, the cheese melting into the ham. This is where the peripheral is blending with the mainstream, where students have different relationships with their professors, where buyers and suppliers behave differently, where patients Google their symptoms before visiting the doctor.

#12: Simple silence

Our senses are working overtime. Looking for a premium-priced luxury product for the next decade or longer? Think simplicity. Picasso drew a dove in eight seconds with just one line when he was 80. Only a master can simplify. Think space. In China it doesn't matter where you travel, you will see people. In the urban age, the space to think and move is a rarity. People yearn for contemplative solitude. Think silence. iPods, mobile phones, cars, voices, music. The relentless cacophony of urban living takes its toll. The art of escapology will become the art of survival. We are all Houdini.

#13: Media is material

One hundred years ago, artists and painters worked with paints and pigments, charcoal and pastels. Materials change. Today's artists are as adept at manipulating images in Photoshop as their predecessors were skilled with brushes. They tinker with pixels. They digitise. Is there anything intrinsically inferior in what they create? No. Beauty is beauty. Art must be art. Now, apply the same thinking to business. Today, organisations have a wealth of new materials to acquire and manipulate in pursuit of temporary monopolies. They can play with the pixels or stick with the pastels. The choice is theirs, but there is a choice.

#14: Self-assembly lives

Things just got personal. Freedom is the new unstoppable virus. Look at the rise of microfinance in some of the poorest countries in the world. Thanks to people like Mohammad Yunus, some of the economically disenfranchised can now take their rightful place in the economic world. More and more of us are loosening the mental shackles. Choice rules. The old ways of living have been abandoned – in Europe, Asia and the Americas. Traditional institutions no longer accept responsibility for us. Welfare institutions are being dismantled through neglect or through political dogma. Their decline is a fact of life – which even higher taxes could not put right.

More freedom equals more responsibility. If you do not make choices, someone else, somewhere else, will make them for you. And you can be sure that they will not care too much about your well-being. We are alone. The new Welfare Society – because this time it is a society rather than a state - is designed by IKEA. It comes in self-assembly flat packs and, as you may have noticed, there are no assembly instructions.

#15: Soul food
More freedom implies more responsibilities for taking care of those around us. As Charles Handy has noted, the market – the dominant institution of our times – is not a substitute for responsibility, merely a mechanism for sorting the efficient from the inefficient. A number of business bestsellers which heavily criticise market capitalism and global brands have appeared since *Funky Business*. Anti-capitalist protests indicate a growing frustration with the institutional arrangements currently in place. They also, largely, miss the point. Global market capitalism is not a political ideology. It is neither good nor bad, right nor wrong – it just is.

Market capitalism is a machine. But a machine does not have a soul. We have to develop the soulful accompaniments to global capitalism as we go along. We need to realise that technological development necessitates changes in our institutions and in our values. If there are no such changes, technological progress will not produce the financial, emotional and human value we anticipated. The so-called digital divide is not a consequence of the technology as such, but rather of our inability to create a world where more people are given an opportunity to develop their talents.

#16: E-(motional) Business

The key idea introduced in *Funky Business*, and one that we still firmly believe in, is that the way to trick the trap of the market is to appeal to the emotional human being – not the rational one. Our time is emotional. We no longer believe unquestionably in science. Scepticism took over, after a century of pure scientific faith, when things began to happen which we had been told were all but impossible – Chernobyl, AIDS, the Ebola virus and so on. When science can no longer provide reassuring answers there is only one thing left: what you can *feel*.

And so, true competitiveness must be built around something we all know exists but which is seldom discussed in the business world: emotions and imagination. Steve Jobs of Apple was asked about what makes the new Mac OS X operating system so great. He replied: 'We made the buttons on the screen look so good you'll want to lick them.' Not a single word about megaHertz and gigabytes. Our senses are working overtime.

So, the question most companies need to ask themselves today is: do we love – not like or fancy, LOVE – our products, colleagues and customers? Are they passionate about you? The real acid test: during the past two years, how many of your customers have tattooed your brand on one of their biceps? If Harley Davidson can get its tribal followers to do it – why can't everyone else? Sounds too fuzzy and touchy-feely? Well, research in neuroscience shows that the brain's limbic system, which governs our feelings, is way more powerful than the neocortex that controls intellect. The traffic instructions that evolution provided our brains with are pretty clear: emotions have the right of way. Logic just has to wait.

#17: Grey spreads

We all just got older. The over-sixties are the new over-thirties. Is your organisation grey aware? The wrinklies now have crinklies; dollar bills burning holes in their brim-full wallets.

#18: RIP Inc.

Where does this leave the standard business corporation?
Answer: the corporation as construed and constructed
throughout the last century is as extinct as a Norwegian blue
in a Monty Python sketch. SOS Inc. The limited company was
set up in response to the fact that we needed capital to utilise
the full potential of new technologies. The beauty of it was that
by minimising individual risk, we maximised risk-taking. But
what if capital is no longer the limited resource it used to be?
Don't we need a new institution?

Technology now enables global, self-organising systems
like Linux and *The Sims*. Elements of self-organisation are
visible in the business models of Amazon and eBay.
Organisational experiments abound, but perhaps even more
important are the institutional implications. If knowledge and
ideas are the most critical assets today, why should those who
control them hand over any proceeds from their economic
value to someone who can only contribute with 'stupid' money?
In capital-intensive industries, yes, but in other cases we need
to come up with an institutional innovation that helps
maximise knowledge creation. The Internet opens the way for
an interpersonal barter economy where we trade services and
experiences. The fact that this stuff cannot be taxed also
brings the new role of government to the forefront.
Technological innovation has always necessitated institutional
innovation and will continue to do so.

#19: The you in network

The rise and rise of social networking and created-by-the-
customer business models is an incredibly powerful and
interesting phenomenon. Co-production is the thing. Mr
Potatohead meets Ryanair by way of IKEA. No wonder we were
all elected person of the year by *Time* magazine in 2006. Look
at YouTube and MySpace, and a whole new world and language
appears. These networks are there thanks to technology, but
they also exist because we have a deep and largely unfulfilled
need for a sense of community. 'In Western societies, at least,

there is a deep and deepening disenchantment with the able role-player or, worse still, the skilled apparatchik – of the political or corporate kind. We are increasingly suspicious that we are being "worked". The search for authenticity is ever more pressing,' say Rob Goffee and Gareth Jones in their book, *Why Should Anyone Be Led By You?* 'There is evidence of the desire for authenticity all around us in popular culture. The seemingly inexorable rise of reality TV (a truly Orwellian phrase as participants are manipulated for an anonymous and isolated audience of voyeurs) is one manifestation. Or we can watch soap operas portraying a nostalgic view of communities – filling the gap left by the decline in genuinely communal life. These questions about authenticity are related to a wider set of concerns about how we live now.' We all want to belong and to overcome the lack of community– as portrayed so powerfully in Robert Putnam's *Bowling Alone*. This human need offers one of the great challenges and opportunities of our times.

These are some of the things we have observed and learned since *Funky Business* appeared. We hope that *Funky Business Forever* provides you, too, with some inspiration to observe and learn. If so, please let us know where it takes you.

Kjell Nordström and Jonas Ridderstråle
June 2007

FUNKY BUSINESS

FUNKY
TIMES

'A working class hero is something to be'
John Lennon

1

We have won. This is the age of capitalist triumph. We have conquered the world from Beijing to Baltimore; St Petersburg to Singapore. Western political leaders can barely conceal their smiles as they tour new stock exchanges in what were once outposts of Communist might. The eyes of business people glaze over with self-congratulatory pride when they are introduced to Chinese entrepreneurs who have made fortunes overnight, or Russian oligarchs who own British football teams. They drool at the emergence of Indian multinationals. Even North Korea's Kim Jong Il is coming round to the big idea of capitalism. Since the fall of the Berlin Wall, triumphalism has been in the air. Capitalism *über alles*.

Thankfully and funkfully, planned economies are an endangered species. Think of the image of the polar bear trapped on a slowly diminishing piece of ice as the surrounding water heats up. Climate change in our societies is an inconvenient truth (to paraphrase Al Gore) for gentlemen such as Kim Jong.

There is one small problem. Karl Marx was right.

We should all catch the first plane to Heathrow, get in a cab and request Highgate Cemetery. There, under an ivy-covered monument, lie the decaying remains of the author of the *Communist Manifesto*, the Communist theorist, Karl Marx. A

This one line has got us into more trouble than any other and helps explain why, despite sweeping the rest of the world, *Funky Business* sold an embarrassing handful of copies in the United States. American audiences find it difficult to move beyond this point of the book. If you are American we entreat you to carry on.

steady stream of visitors comes to the cemetery to view the last resting-place of the great man. Elsewhere in the world, crowds flock to view the decaying remains of Marx's disciples. We, too, should pay homage.

We should pay homage to Ho Chi-Minh. He may be in a crystal coffin in Hanoi with a controlled environment of 60 per cent humidity and 22 degrees Centigrade, but he has the consolation that he was right. The same goes for Vladimir Illich Lenin. Every 18 months he has a bath and is lowered into a mixture of water, alcohol, glycerine and potassium acetate. Two weeks later, his skin is as soft as a baby's bottom. Some 80 years after his death, Lenin's mausoleum is no more than a

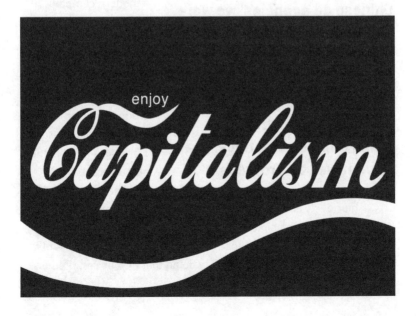

enjoy
Capitalism

tourist attraction for capitalist comrades from the West. Yet, in spite of such indignities and ironies, Lenin was right. As was Chairman Mao Zedong. Mao is now marketed with free market abandon – for a mere 50,000 Hong Kong dollars you can buy a 24-carat golden statue of the great helmsman from the Sing Kwong Jewelry & Gold Co. Place your orders for Erich Honeker teasets and Enver Hoxha memorabilia now. They were all dirty communist dictators, but they were also right.

They were right because they subscribed to the Marxist view that the workers should own the major assets of society, the critical means of production. We now do – though we do so individually rather than collectively. And, perhaps, we did all along but we just didn't have the insight to realise it.

Workers control the principal means of production. The Revolution Part 1 is over. Workers – people in software houses in Frankfurt; shipyard workers in Stavanger; creatives in Chinese ad agencies; suits in offices in Sydney; factory workers in Los Angeles; derivative traders in Singapore – use their brains and, sometimes, their brawn to create new wealth. In a modern company 70 to 80 per cent of what people do – often more – is now done by way of their intellects. The critical means of production is small, grey and weighs around 1.3 kilograms. It is the human brain.

How the world has changed. When we wrote 'Creatives in Chinese ad agencies' we were actually being imaginative and, dare we say it, a little wacky. And yet, it has come to pass: there are great Chinese ad agencies and there are funky Chinese creatives. That is what we call progress.

The human brain is gloriously complex and intricate. It uses holographic organising principles – the parts reflect the whole. Laboratory research even shows that you can take away nine-tenths of a brain and it will still work. Try doing that to your car, iPod or sat nav.

Our brain is capable of outperforming the most powerful computer on earth. Some of you may draw our attention to the chess battle between the IBM chess computer, Deep Blue, and the human Gary Kasparov. In February 1996, didn't the computer eventually beat the human grandmaster? It did, but the victory was possible because both players adhered to the rules, the given number of possible strategies. The trouble for corporate chess players is that future competitiveness will not be about following rules. It will be about breaking old rules and making new ones. Future success will be about challenging current wisdom and moving your pawn from A2 to E7 in one move. Future success will be about solving Fermat's last theorem through creating your own rules.

It seems that John F. Kennedy was also right – even now when the computing power on Planet Earth is estimated to be larger than our assembled brain power – when he said that 'Man is still the most extraordinary computer of all'. People can be creative, come up with new ideas, invent new rules and sense emotions; computers cannot – yet!

Baghdad Bob can tell you that black is indeed white

Ten years later even the coolest-looking Apple computer with all the gigabytes any human being could possibly want is still dumb.

While the human brain is celebrated as the most wonderfully designed, incredibly intricate mechanism, the matter of who actually owns it is blissfully simple. It is not controlled by shareholders, investment funds, or any other body. George Soros may be able to destabilise currencies and markets, but he has no control over your brain. Baghdad Bob can tell you that black is indeed white, but you don't have to believe him. Governments can issue all the propaganda in the world, but your brain is your own. It is controlled, for better or worse, by the individual.

THE BATTLE OF BRAINS

Perfectly formed and individually owned, the human brain is overpowering the traditional means of production – raw material, hard labour and capital. Try to think of one major, successful contemporary business organisation that is brawn based. Even the Mafia and the Hells Angels are now driven more with brainpower than with brutality and horsepower.

Not a carmaker. Manufacturing cars competitively in the new millennium is concerned with utilising technology to manage logistics; to design and manufacture great products; to provide service support; and to communicate internally as well as with networks of suppliers and consumers. Value no longer resides

Henry Ford is often celebrated for his invention of the five-dollar day. This is usually referred to as a glorious act of capitalist benevolence. Highly unlikely we suspect. Old Henry's thinking was impeccably capitalist: greed was good and higher wages meant it was more likely they'd buy the cars.

in the metal or the engine. Instead, value lies with the intangible elements. Some 70 per cent of the value of a new car lies in the intangibles. The result is that the brawniest car producer will be the bankrupt car producer. Car manufacturing is not about mindless, repetitious tasks carried out on a production line. Henry Ford is long dead and so are his methods. Ford once lamented, 'How come when all I want is just a pair of hands I get a human being as well?'. Now, most successful companies are more likely to ask – who needs hands?

Jack Welch, former head of General Electric, once predicted that GE Capital could amount to 50 per cent of the company – not in terms of employees, office buildings and parking lots, but in terms of profits. Why did the undisputed king of heavy industry turn soft? Because nowadays the really hard stuff is the soft stuff.

Entire countries increasingly compete on the basis of knowledge. If you think back, all countries became rich through a combination of natural resources, labour and capital. Think forward and these factors are no longer relevant. In our age, you cannot earn money from natural resources alone. Even the pope agreed. In his 1991 centesimus writings, Pope John Paul II concluded: 'At one time the decisive factor of production was the land, and later capital... Today the decisive factor is man himself, that is, his knowledge.' Business success is, as a result, a matter of herding flocks of brains.

Jack Welch's retirement endeavours – marriage to the former editor of the *Harvard Business Review* whom he got to know rather too closely at an interview and a string of saccharine self-help bestsellers – should not detract from what he stood for: straight talking, results driven, hard-working, a blue collar in the ultimate white-collar job. Welch is the Springsteen of the corporate world.

It doesn't matter whether we are talking about Thailand, Germany, Turkey, the United States or Chile, primacy of knowledge is the only thing we are left to compete with. Natural resources, labour and capital are rapidly diminishing in importance. Look at Dubai: no oil, but lots of talent. That's

Strangely we heard little from Harvard MBA graduate George W. Bush on knowledge.

why Bill Clinton and Tony Blair talked about a 'cold knowledge war'. They were determined to create conditions facilitating brain gain rather than brain drain. The Cold War of the post-war years was about brawn – as symbolised by lines of tanks rumbling past the Kremlin; the new cold war is more subtle (it comes in lower case for a start), but equally crucial – it is brains battling brains.

Battle of Brains

The Third Knowledge Revolution

Knowledge is power is a neat aphorism. It has been used for decades in a loose and vague sort of way. We said it, and we may have said it repeatedly and loudly, but, however loud we shouted, there was the underlying belief that it really wasn't true – the reality was that force was power or, perhaps, power determined what was considered as knowledge. Now, knowledge really is power. We can shout it *and* believe it. Use all the force you want. Bludgeon down walls; threaten and cajole. It won't get you anywhere if you are dealing with someone who is smarter, quicker and hungrier. A nimble lightweight will always beat a ponderous heavyweight – except in the boxing ring. Neanderthal man is long gone; now, we must bid farewell to Neanderthal behaviour and thinking.

Sceptics might say that the role of knowledge in moneymaking activities is nothing new. They would be right. In 1452, mankind saw the dawn of the first knowledge revolution. Johann Gutenberg's invention of the printing press made information more widely available than ever before. Some 500 years later we were hit by the second wave when radio and television began to dominate our lives. Fantastically, the early 1990s marked the beginning of the third wave. As *Time* magazine put it, instead of 500 TV channels, we now have millions of websites. And they are interactive, two-way and live.

One of the interesting things about the even more recent Iraq War is that the best military minds are not necessarily planning battlefield strategy. Instead, they're dealing with the media. Leading the American media offensive was Brigadier General Vincent Brooks, one of the US Army's brightest officers and, according to one report, 'a master of both vivid description and impenetrable obfuscation'.

The scale and speed of the third knowledge revolution is what makes it so different. It is calculated that some 90 per cent of all scientists that have ever walked the face of earth are alive right now. When the US Army fought the Vietnam War, only 15 per cent of the soldiers had a college degree. During Operation Desert Storm, approximately 99.3 per cent of the soldiers were college graduates.

But beware; articulated knowledge is increasingly becoming a commodity. MBAs around the world all read the same books, so do architects and engineers. What used to be sufficient to know is now merely necessary. If something can be communicated orally or written down in a mail or an article it can also be transmitted. And what can be easily diffused is also easily copied.

Knowledge is the new battlefield for countries, corporations and individuals. We all increasingly face conditions that demand more knowledge for us to function and, in the long run, for us to survive. You can't build a wall around knowledge. You can't isolate it. It is there. It is in the air; in cyberspace. It envelops the human race.

The Internet makes almost anything available to anyone, anywhere and anytime. It is gloriously (and worryingly at times) independent of time, space and device. If knowledge is power, power now potentially resides everywhere. The scale of the changes, and of the opportunities, makes this a genuine revolution. In such times we are all condemned

An interesting footnote is that Socrates is strangely fashionable in business literature. Socratic discussion and questioning is in. We are all ears.

to be perpetually un(der)-educated. Or as Socrates once said: 'I know nothing except the fact of my own ignorance.'

The revolutionary manifesto moves around the world with frightening speed. Once you could have a monopoly on knowledge, as an individual or a company, for a fairly long period of time. If a company had a smart idea in 1950, it took a while for others to jump on the bandwagon or even to find out. The archetypal firms of the early and mid-twentieth century were companies like the UK glassmaker Pilkington; the South African mining company De Beers; and the American giant, Xerox. These companies often had as long as 20 or even 30 years to exploit globally their firm-specific advantages – the stuff that made them unique. They could use an incremental and sequential internationalisation process, gradually adding nation after nation. They conquered Argentina, then moved on to Peru and so on. The world could be inexorably dominated.

This is no longer the case. Today, knowledge spreads internationally and instantly. Business best practice moves faster than ever before. Business schools and universities spread the word with remorseless efficiency. In the 1960s, US business schools graduated some 5,000 MBA students per year. Today, that figure is 75,000. Back in 1967, two such MBA programmes existed in the UK. In 2006, 152 programmes were up and running. In the US, there are now around 800. Just in the United States, there are nearly half a million MBA students, and that number should reach a million by 2012. Around 100,000 MBA graduates are let loose on the world every year. As they nurse their graduation hangover, they might like to contemplate the fact that much of their knowledge is already out of date.

Knowledge spreads. The Danish hearing-aid company Oticon launched a different way of organising itself – project organisation instead of regular hierarchy, no papers, new office architecture, etc. It was innovative and imaginative. Jack Welch of GE launched the concept of a boundaryless organisation – transforming the whale into a shoal of dolphins. Before long, such bright ideas are written up in case studies. Organisations benchmark. They look around. Word spreads. Other companies copy Oticon and GE. Like some deadly virus, once knowledge is out there, it cannot be stopped.

REVOLUTIONS REVISITED

The fact that Karl Marx and his dictatorial disciples were right does not mean that we are reconstituted Communists. While they were right, they were far from entirely right. Indeed, they may only have been right about one small thing. If you look around, the rich have never been wealthier. If you look around, capitalism has rarely looked healthier.

Of course, not everyone agrees with this view of the world. Complacency is easily found. Before he fell sick, in one of his execrable and lengthy sermons the Cuban leader Fidel Castro informed his long-suffering people that they were going through *un periodo especial*. Castro promised that normal service (or lack of service if you are Cuban) would be resumed shortly. Castro advised his people to sit tight, wait, and relax. They are probably still waiting – and now with some apprehension for his successor. Revolutionary zeal has turned into wishful thinking.

Like it or not, change cannot be turned on and off. At the moment it is pouring uncontrollably. Put your hand over it and the water will spread in all directions. Sit back and you will drown. Welcome to the real revolution, Fidel.

At the time of going to press there was some uncertainty surrounding the state of health of Castro who had rarely been seen in public since ceding power to his brother Raul following surgery in mid-2006.

The reality is that the revolution we are currently experiencing is bigger even than that imagined by Marx. It is a revolution that will change the very nature of our societies, economies, industries, firms, jobs and personal lives. It is all-embracing. And it is happening now. You may not be able to see barricades in the street and tear gas filling the air, but it is happening – in your and our minds.

In all likelihood you have never experienced a revolution. Nor have we. (We are Swedish after all.) But we know that during revolutions you throw out the rulebook. Revolutions are lawless, spontaneous and dangerous. We are not suggesting you begin looting, but pointing out that in this new environment there are no rules, there are no laws, nothing is given. There is constant motion – perpetual crises. Traditional roles, jobs, skills, ways of doing things, insights, strategies, aspirations, fears and expectations no longer count.

Herb Kelleher did just that at Southwest Airlines. He set fire to it. Greg Dyke did much the same at the BBC. His rule-eliminating initiative was engagingly called 'Cut the crap'. Unfortunately, thanks to the deadly spectre of politics, Greg didn't cut it at the BBC.

In this environment we cannot have business as usual. We need business as *unusual.* We need different business. We need innovative business. We need unpredictable business. We need surprising business. We need funky business.

Funky Business Is Truly Global

No kidding this time. Internationalisation has gone through a number of false dawns. Now it is the real thing. There are no borders for Luciano Pavarotti or the Kaiser Chiefs, a band from Yorkshire in the UK, named after a South African soccer team, who opened Live in Philadelphia. Madonna feels no borders. Lenovo does not care about nation states. Terrorism cuts across the globe and you have to carry your toothpaste in a plastic bag at the airport.

Terrorism makes you pack a plastic bag

15

And, we have never seen a larger economic space. During the past 40 years, international trade has increased by 1,500 per cent. No wonder, when average tariffs have

The most recent figures: total merchandise trade of exports was worth 58,000 million in 1948 and 10,431,000 million in 2005 – that's US dollars at current prices.

simultaneously been slashed. We travel the world and the seven seas. We have global satellite channels, international magazines, TV shows, movies, hit-records, etc. The global village envisaged by Marshall McLuhan in the 1960s is here.

Capitalism is on the move. Look at Eastern Europe and the former Soviet Union. There are more than 30 new nations in the UN since the Wall fell – such as Belarus, Ukraine and Georgia. Some are poor but want Western affluence as quickly as possible. So, they have been exporting madly. They export pulp and paper products. They export software. They export chemicals. In fact, they export everything they have. They are cold – freezing to death – and still export coal and oil. They are the new competitors.

Even wealthy Switzerland joined the UN in 2002 after more than 50 years of hesitation.

Many more are joining the throng. In the mid-1990s, outside the OECD there were roughly 200 million people with realistic notions of joining the capitalist march. Countries like Japan, Singapore and Hong Kong were coming up fast. They were within reach. Now, more than 3,000 million people are on the move. OK, we're not actually sure where we got this figure from. The world population is 6.5 billion and how many of them are prepared to chase economic prosperity? Many, many

Since *Funky Business* was published hundreds of thousands of Poles have moved to the UK. Towns like Reading now have a Polish newspaper and fantastic plumbing.

What is staggering is that the figure we used in *Funky Business* was much lower. The population of countries such as India is still on the up – many millions up on even a few years ago.

millions. They come from the Indian sub-continent (1 billion people), the former Soviet Union (145 million), Poland, (39 million), Vietnam (84 million), Pakistan (163 million), Indonesia (246 million) and so on. They are all in the process of building lives and societies similar to those in the West. They would like the same comfort, material possessions and decadence. They will achieve their objectives. It is simply a question of when.

What is staggering is that the figures we used in *Funky Business* were much lower. The population of countries such as India is still on the up – many millions up on even a few years ago. In India, 20 per cent of the people already have the same standard of living as the average European (in purchasing power parity terms). In 2006, 22 per cent of Indians lived under the poverty line. An awful statistic, we know, but down from 50 per cent in 1995. At this moment, in Bangalore, 140,000 IT engineers are at work. Bangalore is now the world's second largest city for software development. Novell is there. Siemens is there. Ericsson is there. In fact, more than 20 per cent of the *Fortune 500* companies are there.

Multinationals are not in India for charitable purposes. Think how much these Indian engineers earn. The answer is something like $1,000 a month. Why would you hire anyone from Sweden, Germany, France or the US, when Indian engineers work so cheaply and the quality of their work is identical to that found in our supposedly advanced societies? The economics could not be simpler; the ramifications could not be more profound.

So tough is the competition from the experts of Bangalore and beyond that some of the most prestigious US universities – including Stanford, Berkeley and UCLA – already operate a quota system to limit the number of non-American students.

The stark truth is that, competing on grades alone, many US students would not stand a chance against their Asian fellows. Limiting this talent pool has been questioned by authors like Richard Florida. Without a flow of students from abroad the US might become less innovative over time, he anticipates.

In the global village we can't do it alone. Sisters and brothers simply can't do it for themselves. We need to find world-class partners. We need the best – the best architect, the best supplier, the best consultant – rather than the closest. This is already happening. The Ford Focus is produced by factories in: Saarlouis, Germany; Valencia, Spain; Santa Rosa, Laguna, Philippines; Pacheco, Argentina; Chongqing, China; and Wayne, Michigan in the United States. Kits for assembly are supplied to Vsevolzhsk near St Petersburg, Russia. The economic realities of our time mean that everybody competes with everybody else. All of us are in global competition. Individuals are in global competition. Companies are in global and generic competition. Countries are in global competition. There is nowhere to run and nowhere to hide. For us. For you. For Enron. For Fiat. For U2. For Oprah. For Leo DiCaprio.

The long-tail phenomenon is not simply a neat idea for a book, it's happening. The category 'others' is growing in most industries. Now, it can be incredibly profitable to target small groups of consumers.

Funky Business Means More Competition for Everything Everywhere

In the West we have been brought up with the belief that more is good. This is not necessarily true. But more is certainly evident wherever you look. More products; more markets; more people; more competition. More is a fact of life.

In 1996 at the Atlanta Olympics, Sweden won two gold medals. When the medalists returned to Stockholm, they held

FUNKY BUSINESS

a press conference at the airport. One medal winner pointed out that athletes from 53 nations took the 271 gold medals on offer at Atlanta. Four years earlier in Barcelona, 37 countries won gold medals. She predicted that at the Sydney Olympics in 2000, 80 or 90 nations

She was wrong. Only 51 nations did, but the point is still valid. It is becoming harder and harder to win gold in athletics or car production.

would be able to win a gold medal. If you are an athlete you don't know where the competition is going to come from next.

A similar rule applies elsewhere. Even the hallowed and sheltered halls of academia are not immune. We taught at the Stockholm School of Economics. At the time we worked there, in some years there were 5,000 applicants for just 300 places. Those who succeeded in getting into the school had the highest grades in every single subject, truly Renaissance men and women. The School was founded at the beginning of the twentieth century to educate the elite of the elite. Twenty or so years ago, if you were Swedish and interested in business administration and economics, our school was the only real choice. The same was largely true just five years ago.

Now, bright, 20-year-old Scandinavians look around. They look at the Universität zu Köln, Ashridge in the UK, SDA Bocconi in Italy, INSEAD in France, Duke University in North Carolina. They weigh up the pros and cons. They compare the schools. Stockholm used to be the only choice, now it is one of more than 1,000. And things will only get worse – or better – depending on who you are. The net will spread so that students automatically consider (so far unbuilt) Asian business schools or even schools in cyberspace.

There are now more than 1,000 MBA programmes to choose from in India. Alternatively, you can obtain a perfectly acceptable MBA if you stay in Lapland, buy a PC, read your Michael Porter assiduously and never leave home.

MBA = Mediocre But Arrogant

We are moving towards what academics call techno-economic parity. Techno-economic parity implies that there

Tom Friedman probably liked our metaphor when he wrote his book _The World is Flat_. The Economist recently noted the world is bumpy.

are very few commodities, technologies, products, services, insights, knowledge areas or procedures in London, Paris, New York, Milan and Madrid that are not also available to our friends, brothers and sisters in Bangalore, Seoul, Gdansk, Buenos Aires and Kuala Lumpur. Techno-economic parity also implies that the basic prerequisites for doing business are becoming flatter by the day. The playing field once had a slope as steep as Mont Blanc. Now it is being forced to the horizontal. In essence, techno-economic parity means that the best man or woman wins, no matter where they come from. The industrialised world no longer has a knowledge monopoly because knowledge moves freely. So we all need to prepare for the 'Business Olympics'. This event is not held every four years. It is happening now – in real time, non-stop.

Now, bright, 20-year-old Scandinavians look around

Funky Business Requires a Creative Search for Differentiation

In the wild market economy which now exists it is increasingly difficult to differentiate yourself. If you think about it, most of what your business does could be bought from someone else using the Yellow Pages or Google. If you have a unique idea your competitors will steal it in two or three weeks. With three billion people in the process of building lives and societies similar to our own, competitive pressures are reaching boiling point. And they will keep on simmering.

There is only one way out. It is deceptively simple: stop the karaoke and do something else; do something that the world has not seen before. Innovate so that you are, for a moment in time, unique and uniquely competitive.

But, be warned, you will have to be unique in new ways. The old way of achieving uniqueness was to add a few extras to your product. This no longer works – it will be copied within days, perhaps hours, and consumers are no longer so easily fooled.

Organisations, services and products are becoming more and more similar. Often, you need a microscope to spot the differences. In the United States, the car industry waits

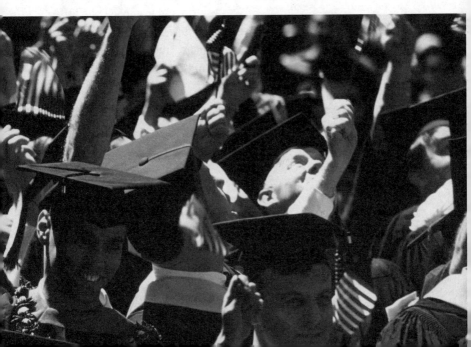

expectantly for reports from the rating institute, JD Power. Its final report for a recent year began with the observation that 'There are no bad cars any longer, because they are all good'. The car companies, whether they are Audi, Toyota, Ford or Renault, understand all the technology at their disposal. They understand each other's products. They take them apart and examine their innermost workings. Differentiation in the car industry must, therefore, come from other areas.

The new competitive battlefield is not the engine or the air conditioner – it is the design, the warranty, the service deal, the image and the finance package. Intelligence and intangibles. Emotions. And, of course, people. People can make your organisation, your products and your service solutions unique. How you manage and lead people, how you organise your operations, will determine whether or not you succeed.

As a result, we need to rethink our definition of what is really valuable. According to the *Economist*, the new acid test is whether it hurts when you drop your competitive advantage on your toes. If it does, you should start rethinking the way in which you operate. Things that were in demand used to consist of a little knowledge and a lot of stuff. The new valuables are made up of a little stuff and a lot of knowledge. Stuff it! The average weight of a real dollar's worth of US exports has more than

Some things stay the same: This was true in 1999 and it is still less than half.

Fast or forgotten

halved since 1970. The density of a successful customer offering is changing. Today, competitive advantages weigh no more than the dreams of a butterfly.

Funky Business Requires Organisational Innovation

Organising is the art of achieving extraordinary things with ordinary people. In our times, organisational innovation means creating conditions that enable a constant flow of creativity, not the churning out of yet another standardised product or service. Funky firms need to be different, look different, and work in new ways. They are all on a quest to discover a new organisational model or mind-set.

All modern companies compete on knowledge, but knowledge is perishable. We must treat it like fresh milk – we have to date it. Unless we use the knowledge of our firm it becomes sour and loses its value. Continuous innovation, both revolutionary and evolutionary, is a necessity. Or, as David Vice famously put it when he was CEO at Northern Telecom: 'In the future there will be two kinds of companies – the quick and the dead.' We are either fast or forgotten. In the new economy, there are no speed limits. Agility rules. Speed is all. The need for renewal is something that applies to everything in the organisation; it concerns everyone; goes on everywhere; and is non-stop. 'We intend to move as fast as we can, ripping up the road behind us,' says Intel's Craig Barrett. And he means it. Look around and the advice is simple:

Move it. In a single year, 1,000 new soft-drinks were launched on the Japanese market. A year later, one per cent was still for sale.

More controversially, in recent years the company has applied the same discipline to the employment of its CEOs.

Move it faster. At Hewlett-Packard, a majority of revenues come from products that did not exist a year ago.

Move it now. In Tokyo, you can order a customised Toyota on Monday and be driving it on Friday.

Funky Business Puts Management and Leadership Centre Stage

Leadership and management are more important than ever before. Gurus and commentators have been proclaiming this for years, maybe because it justified their existence. Now it is reality.

This is the age of time and talent, where we are selling time and talent, exploiting time and talent, organising time and talent, hiring time and talent, packaging time and talent. The most critical resource wears shoes and walks out the door around five o'clock every day. As a result, management and leadership are keys to competitive advantage. They differentiate you from the mass. How you attract, retain and motivate your people is more important than technology; how you treat your customers and suppliers, more

Talent = Intellectual capital + Social capital + Psychological capital. To succeed in making financial capital dance you need know-how and know-who, plus a can-do attitude. So, the smart thing to do is to enhance your competencies, develop your community and to be courageous.

important than technology. How a company is managed and how a company is led are vital differentiators. They can create uniqueness. But at the same time as management and leadership have reached maturity as potent competitive weapons, their very nature has changed.

The boss is dead. The executive dinosaur – witness David Brent in *The Office* – is officially extinct. (Obviously, members of the species are usually the last to realise that their days are numbered.) No longer can we believe in a leader who claims to know more about everything and who is always right. Management by numbers is history. Management by fear won't work. If management is people, management must become *humanagement*.

We are not suggesting that everyone who wears shoes is a critical resource. It's the right people. Also remember that seen from the firm's perspective, the wrong people are liabilities, not assets.

The job is dead. No longer can we believe in having a piece of paper saying job description at the top. The new realities call for far greater flexibility. Throughout most of the twentieth century, managers averaged one job and one career. Now, we are talking about two careers at least and seven jobs or more.

The days of the long-serving corporate man, safe and sound in the dusty recesses of the corporation, are long gone. Soon, the emphasis will be on getting a life instead of a career, and work will be viewed as a series of gigs or projects.

Inevitably, new roles demand new skills. Thirty years ago, we had to learn one new skill per year. Now, it is one new skill per day. Tomorrow, it may be one new skill per hour. Skills like networking – in 1960, the average manager had to learn 25 names throughout his or her entire career; today we must learn 25 new names every single month. Tomorrow, it may be 25 new names per week (and half of those are likely to be names from different languages).

Funky Business gives us the Power

No jobs but more power. We now own the major assets of society – our own minds. And power equals freedom. We are all potentially free to know, go, do and be whoever we want to be. We choose. We can be picky. It is up to us. But freedom is not something you are simply handed. It is something you conquer. And, today, power lies in controlling the scarcest of resources: human intelligence.

Free at last! But we are also in the midst of a great freedom hangover. People are beginning to realise that with freedom come responsibilities. This is our take on it, however. Never forget that while freedom can be good and bad, the absence of freedom can only be bad.

The more unique we are – the better we will do. And as opposed to physical resources, knowledge grows with usage and is portable – you can take it with you when you leave. So, if you really want to build a good life – and/or just make money – the route to success couldn't be clearer: get at it and get going. The power is yours to use and abuse.

INTO THE FUNKY FUTURE

With the introduction of the plantation we moved from the hunting and gathering society into the agricultural one and, with the coming of electricity, we entered the industrial era. Lenin once said that Communism equals Soviet power plus electrification of the entire country. Funkyism equals information mania plus the power of choice. Some call our world the knowledge society and others the brain-based one. The only thing certain is that the critical skills and answers of tomorrow will not be those of today. More important, however, may be the fact that the relevant questions are changing. Paradoxically, the ability to forget – unlearning – is becoming a key asset in a business world changing at the speed of light.

Change then change again. We are facing a world of chaos and genuine uncertainty. The new realities have been pithily described by Kent Foster, now the CEO of Ingram Micro, as: 'Products that are still evolving, delivered to a market that is still emerging, via a technology that is still changing on a daily basis.' It won't slow down for you to understand what is going on or to take a snapshot. In such a world, the only thing that we can trust is that the certain becomes uncertain, and the unlikely becomes likely.

The future cannot be predicted – it is to be created. Either you see things happen or you make them happen. You may be tempted to categorise the ideas and trends discussed in this book as good or bad, black or white. Resist temptation. Evolution is not right or wrong – it just is. We may use electricity to kill people or to make toast. Electricity is. The Internet can be used to distribute child pornography or to

Bill Clinton is no longer in office and his semantic difficulties pale against those of the Bush administration. As ex-Defence Secretary Donald Rumsfeld put it so eloquently: 'Reports that say that something hasn't happened are always interesting to me because as we know, there are known knowns; there are things we know we know. We also know there are known unknowns; that is to say we know there are some things we do not know. But there are also unknown unknowns – the ones we don't know we don't know.' Similarly, Henry Kissinger is reputed to have walked into a press conference and said, 'Does anyone have any questions for my answers?' Welcome to the knowledge economy!

FUNKY BUSINESS

meet your future spouse. The Internet is. The future does not exist. It is not good or bad. It becomes what we make it. 'What is *is*,' says the Dalai Lama (while Bill Clinton laboured over the exact meaning of is). Funky *is*.

Funky business means there will be many more questions with fewer and fewer answers. Einstein was wrong. No single theory can guide us. Diversity rules. Questions rather than answers

What is is

fundamentally drive the future. And along the way, do not expect any help from technology, because, as Pablo Picasso once pointed out: 'Computers are useless. They can only give us answers.' But, if you ask smart questions, in a unique way, faster than anyone else, you will be momentarily ahead of the game. Enjoy it. Seconds later you have to think of the next question. Then the next.

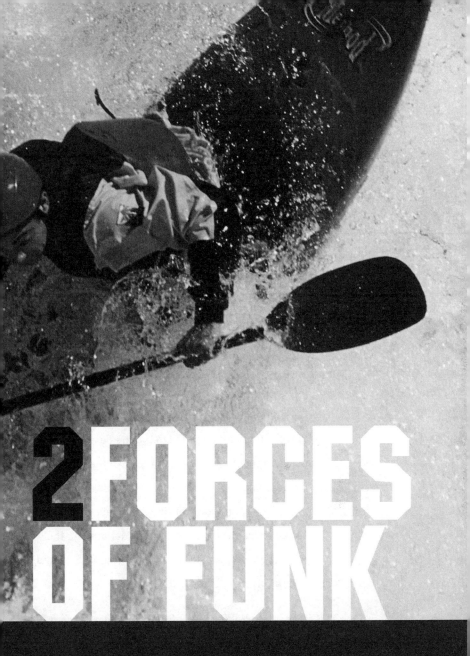

2 FORCES OF FUNK

'I am the trouble starter — punkin' instigator'
The Prodigy

If you are in danger of underestimating the new funky world, simply recite a selection of the facts below. Expect the unexpected. Forget fact-checkers, now we need funk-checkers:

1 Gerry Adams of Sinn Fein and archenemy loyalist, the Reverend Ian Paisley, held a press conference together.

2 In 1999, his holiness, Pope John Paul II, launched a CD 'Abbà Pater' on which he rapped. In a collaborative effort with techno and ambient musicians the pope went pop. Later the Vatican announced the launch of a follow-up CD on which you could listen to the pope's prayers as interpreted by N'Sync and Britney Spears. Ooops, they did it again!

3 The terrorist group die Rote Armee Faktion (Red Army Faction) sent a letter to the media in 1998 declaring that they were closing down their operations. They claimed that there was no longer any fertile ground for their ideas. In February 2007 a Stuttgart court ruled that Brigitte Mohnhaupt, the last of the incarcerated members of the RAF, would be paroled and released.

4 Things definitely got weirder. By the time we came to write *Karaoke Capitalism*, some four years later, we looked at a world where the best rapper was white and the best golfer was black; Larry Flynt, founder of porno-magazine *Hustler*, wanted to become

Governor of California and his main contender in the race was the Terminator – Arnold Schwarzenegger; France accused the US of arrogance; and Denmark sent a mini-submarine to a desert war.

5 God and Mammon finally join hands and make friends. A UK university now offers an MBA in church management.

6 Article 11 of the Chinese constitution has been revised to read: 'Individual, private and other non-public economies that exist within the limits prescribed by law are major components of the socialist market economy.'

7 The GE factory in Louisville, Kentucky, was built in 1953 and has 25,000 parking spaces. Impressive. The problem is that in 1997 the factory only had 10,000 employees and, by 2003, GE employed about 7,600 employees in the whole of Kentucky.

8 Hermes' Grace Kelly bag takes 17 hours to produce and can cost up to $50,000 new. A Hermes Birkin bag (named after British-born actress and singer Jane Birkin, long resident in France) fetched $64,250 at auction in New York and a single artist can spend up to 25 hours painstakingly constructing the bag. Nissan leads auto manufacturers on productivity with 28.24 labour hours per vehicle – just over three hours longer than a Hermes bag.

The world is a stage (and the stage looks like a marketplace). We all play roles – organisations as well as individuals. But instead of conventional costume drama, we now have constant, unscripted, improvised theatre. The director has left,

The constitution goes on to say that, 'The State protects the lawful rights and interests of the individual and private sectors of the economy, and exercises guidance, supervision and control over individual and the private sectors of the economy.'

the original play is cancelled and the script is missing. The spectators are pouring onto the stage, joining the actors, demanding leading roles. Boundaries are blurring. Every role is vacant. Old rules no longer exist – the goodies and the baddies are the same person. Everything is up for grabs.

We are all contributors to the new society developing in front of our eyes. It is horrifying. It is fantastic. It is frightening. It is fun. It is depressing. It is weird. It is the funky village.

And if the world is being propelled headlong down a corridor of endless uncertainty and unceasing surprise, you would be justified in asking what forces are pushing us at the speed of sound. Who closed down the theatre, sacked the director and shredded the script? What has got us into such a funk?

We do not believe there is anything particularly mysterious about the forces behind the revolution we are now witnessing. Revolutions are never

The arch globalist, Kenichi Ohmae's last book was called *The New Global Stage*. Ohmae makes the globalist point by taking visitors to a local supermarket in Tokyo. There the world's products are laid out for all – lemons from Spain, lamb from New Zealand, Italian olives, British sausages and so on. The world is a global stage and we are all tucking into the exotic entrées.

subtle events. Tidiness and order aren't paramount as you storm the palace. At times of radical change, nuances are usually notable by their absence. We believe the three drivers moving us forward into the unknown are changes in technology, institutions and values. None operate in a vacuum. All overlap and interlink. Their impact is on each other as well as on society, companies and individuals.

TECHNOLOGY: THE ENDLESS RIFF

Technology – in the form of biotechnology, nanotechnology, information technology, transportation technology and many other guises – is reshaping our world. Technology is the rhythm section of funky business. Management guru Tom Peters **Companies are beginning to realise that you need to adapt technology to people, rather than the reverse.** provides a pithy summing up of where we now stand: 'The nerds have won.' Welcome to Nerdville.

Technology is not just a matter of nuts and bolts or bits and bytes. It is not a sideshow, but the ultimate in mass participation. It is curious – and a little daunting – to think back just a few decades. In the fifties, sixties and seventies, technology was the domain of the military, rocket scientists, obscure academics and professors working in the R&D departments of pharmaceutical companies. Technology was Nobel laureates, Yuri Gagarin, Apollo, missile systems and radar. Then it became commercialised, hijacked by entrepreneurial geeks. Creators of weapons of mass destruction dumbed down (or *dumbed up*, depending on your prejudices) to become instruments of mass entertainment like games and gambling.

Take the computer company SiliconGraphics. Fifteen years ago this company's most sophisticated customer was the US Army; then it became Mickey Mouse. When SiliconGraphics

It is now possible to replace defective DNA before a baby is born. In vitro fertilization is now reckoned by fertility clinics to be a more reliable, though less pleasurable, method of becoming pregnant than sexual intercourse – we guess this depends on whom you married. Designer sperm is a reality. There is even a sperm bank where donors are Nobel Prize laureates. There is something bizarre about a world in which people first accept an award from the hand of a king and then go to the clinic to use their own hands for an entirely different creative purpose. Artificial wombs are only a few years away. Soon we will be able to build our kids cafeteria style.

gets a new request from the Disney Corporation or Steven Spielberg, the engineers know that their paymaster is on the line. Today, it is movies and computer games rather than missile systems that frequently drive the most sophisticated developments in IT. Similarly, often it is retailers rather than manufacturers who lead the IT way. Software has the upper hand over hardware.

The riff of technology is unstoppable and irresistible. Axiom: technology is changing and will continue to change faster than any government can issue regulations to control it.

The curse of funky? SGI filed for Chapter 11 bankruptcy protection in May 2006, emerging in October 2006. It delisted from NASDAQ in 2005. SGI's former headquarters is now home to Google so there is obviously no bad karma. The restructured SGI has a new business model: the company 'delivers a complete range of high-performance server and storage solutions'.

It is easy to forget how far we have come in such a short space of time. Alvin Toffler, a man with his eyes open to future possibilities and who calls himself a futurist, wrote his best-selling *The Third Wave* in 1980. Look at it now and you will be startled. It was written comparatively recently, yet the technological leaps made since its publication have been immense. Toffler, for example, has to explain what a word processor is – and mentions its alternative labels, 'the smart typewriter' or 'text editor'. He envisages the office of the future: 'The ultimate beauty of the electronic office lies not merely in the steps saved by a secretary in typing and correcting letters. The automated office can file them in the form of electronic bits on tape or disc. It can (or soon will) pass them through an electronic dictionary that will automatically correct their spelling errors. With the machines hooked up to one another and to the phone lines, the secretary can instantly transmit the letter to its recipient's printer or screen.' In 1980, to the vast majority of Toffler's readers this read like science fiction. Now, it is reality to the vast majority of people in the industrialised world (or de-industrialised world, according to Toffler's perspective). To some, it is already dusty history.

Alvin and Heidi Toffler's *Revolutionary Wealth* was written in 2006. It describes the world as high-speed, with its constantly changing, seemingly random impacts on our businesses, governments, families and daily lives. The Tofflers focus their attention on the revolution in wealth now sweeping the planet. Twenty-first century wealth, according to them, is not just about money, and cannot be understood in terms of industrial-age economics. They write about everything from education and childrearing to Hollywood and China, from everyday truth and lies to what they call our 'Third Job' – the unnoticed work we do without pay for some of the biggest corporations.

Digital Data

The central contribution of technology to funky business is in
creating communication and information systems. The impact
of information technology is omnipresent. Today, information
flows freely. You can't avoid it. It's like getting sand in your
swimming trunks – a little annoying and close to impossible to
get rid of.

The rhythm is never ending, like some mystical chant. Beat
after beat. Today, there is far more computing power in the
average car than there was in the first Apollo spacecraft that
took man to the moon. There is more computing power in a
greeting card singing *Happy Birthday* than existed on Planet
Earth back in 1950. One Blu Ray disc has the capacity to store
25 million pages of text. That's around 100,000 *Funky Business*
books. Not so long ago the fax was an important technological
advance. Who now trumpets fax technology? Ditto the electric
typewriter (with memory!). Ditto the floppy disc.

If we were to see the same development in the field of air
travel as that we have witnessed in the IT industry during the
past 25 years, a flight from New York to Scandinavia would not
cost $500 or more and take some eight hours. In fact, by now it
would take under one second and cost less than one cent. The
downside would be that the plane would be tiny and would
crash once a week – trivial matters with such a
price/performance ratio.

The beat goes on. The current wave of digitisation is already
affecting us all. IT development continues to make huge leaps.
Most people in the West have a mobile phone or two. Our
homes may soon be gadget-filled temples of virtual reality –
just like Bill Gates' but smaller.

The momentum is unstoppable for a variety of reasons.
Think, for example, of how little fun it would be if you were the
only one with a mobile phone, the only person with access to
email or if you belonged to a network of one. Ludicrous
perhaps but it does lead to a more significant insight.
'Metcalfe's Law' states that the experienced utility of belonging

We admit that we sometimes gave Mr Gates a hard time in *Funky Business*. He did, at the time, embody a certain kind of nerdy corporate brilliance which we found squeaky clean and consequently a little irritating. His recent work, however, demands that we change our opinions. His philanthropy is magnificent and carefully thought out. Who would have thought that Bill and Warren Buffett would be bracketed together as the great givers of our times? You cannot belittle their generosity, but you can question whether it is a good thing that the health and prosperity of some of the world's most deprived inhabitants should rely on two billionaires. Are we really building a better world?

to an electronic network increases exponentially with the number of users. Put simply, it is more than twice as fun if there are two instead of one.

And then there are three, then four and so on. Once these networks reach critical mass, they explode. It appears such fun to join that people just cannot resist. They spread as remorselessly as ivy. Mobile phones and the Internet demonstrate Metcalfe's Law in practice. It is notable that the dissenting voices about either of these technologies are now rarely, if ever, heard. The Luddite traditionalists who cast the Internet as Big Brother have been silenced – many, no doubt, have signed up and are cruising somewhere in cyberspace. In 2007 Internet usage surpassed gardening as the preferred pastime for pensioners in a UK survey by the AXA insurance company. The Brits are blooming in front of their screens.

Those who continue to be critical usually miss the point: 'Put me in a room with a pad and a pencil and set me up against a hundred people with a hundred computers – I'll outcreate every goddamn sonofabitch in the room,' says the writer Ray Bradbury, mistaking the creative opportunities offered by technology for creativity itself.

The phenomenon of Metcalfe's Law explains why IT converts are so eager to tell their friends to get wired. The more people who join, the more your own cellular phone, Internet connection or website is worth. In 2005 IT entrepreneur Martin Varsavsky founded Fon with the idea that members of the Fon network should share their routers worldwide, thereby creating a free broadband network. A router was promised to members for a nominal sum.

**Moore's Law
+
Metcalfe's Law
+
Coase's Law
=
Hierarchy R.I.P**

Academics usually refer to this as network externalities or the law of increasing returns. Here, old rules no longer apply: value decreases rather than increases with scarcity. Translation: to those who have shall be given (even more). By winning initial advantages or market shares, over time you will benefit from additional positive spin-offs. The more known or used your customer offering is, the more people will want to use it. As a consequence, sooner or later, someone is probably going to start giving away whatever it is you are now selling. Give it away to gain these initial advantages and eventually kill all the others. This Law of 'Give to Gain' was among the 10 promulgated by Kevin Kelly, the founder of *Wired Magazine,* in his book *The New Rules of the New Economy* some years ago.

Digital Dreams

New technology increases both nativity and mortality. Eras come and go. Winners rise and fall. Every now and then, the fundamentals on which society is built erode and our constructions collapse. The old must make room for the new. When shipping became a potent force for the creation of competitive advantage, cities such as Venice and Lisbon flourished. Later, railroads turned these cities into tourist attractions while new junctions became more critical. Then came the automobile. Then the airplane. Just as Petra in the

Middle East lost its position as a leading commercial centre and is now mainly of archaeological interest, digitisation will exterminate some species and enable new ones.

IT decreases time and space. We live in a shrinking world. Cyberspace – once described by author William Gibson as a 'consensual hallucination' – is the seventh continent. We no longer have a workplace; we have a workspace – and a lifespace and the two seem to melt together with time. Our publisher moves his entire office from Stockholm to Majorca to escape the winter. A laptop and printer and a broadband connection are all he needs. Then he moves back with the migrating birds. The new immigrants are virtual ones, taking jobs from someone else without even showing their faces. Instead of moving people, we are beginning to move their thoughts and ideas. It is an entirely new ball game – with entirely new rules. And most organisations do not adapt – they die.

IT enables total transparency. People with access to relevant information are beginning to challenge any type of authority. The stupid, loyal and humble customer, employee and citizen are dead. Voters are challenging politicians; subordinates are challenging managers; students are challenging professors; patients are challenging doctors; kids are challenging parents; customers are challenging companies; and women are challenging men. Anyone whose claim to fame rests on a historical information advantage is challenged – challenged by individuals, organisations and regions with direct access to the same information. It is a power shift. The periphery is becoming the centre. Power now belongs to the people.

Challenge is in the air because the digital world removes the emperor's clothes. It makes George W. Bush transparent, GE transparent, and the UN transparent. And you, too, are transparent. IT enables us to be anonymous – you can build your own personality, cafeteria style, on the Internet. You can be anyone. You can be man or woman, old or young, black or white. You decide. But IT does not make us invisible. On the contrary. We all leave tracks. Every time you surf the net, you leave tracks. Every time you use your credit card, you leave tracks. Every time you make a phone call, you leave tracks. These tracks can be used for multiple purposes. Information can be used to capture criminals or customers – paedophiles or bibliophiles. Whether we like it or not, we are all becoming self-segmenting individuals. Companies, organisations and authorities can find out who else makes similar tracks; people who follow similar trails – our binary and imaginary siblings in cyberspace – and so can we.

Total transparency also has a tendency to reveal and expose those not really adding any value. IT will mean the death of the intermediary as we know him/her – instead we will get infomediaries: information brokers. Infomediaries are people and firms who eliminate unnecessary actors in the value chain by simultaneously functioning as purchase agents for customers and sales departments for sellers. They may be entirely new actors or just existing firms that take on this role themselves. We now routinely buy our airline tickets online and direct from airlines. Why give your money to a travel agent? Why give your money to a wholesaler? Why give your money to a traditional record company? Why turn to retailers when there are e-tailers?

IT perfects markets. In the beginning there were markets. We traded. People exchanged goods for goods, and then

Back in the bazaar

goods for money. Price became the carrier of information. In the local bazaar, all the information was available at your fingertips. You could see, feel and smell the tomatoes, fish, jewellery, or whatever. But, as products got more complex and geographical distances increased, information became scarcer and feedback slower. Uncertainty exploded. Markets began to experience problems.

In response, we began to build hierarchies and formed them into organisations. We made stuff in-house rather than buying it from someone else. Markets and hierarchies basically fulfil the same function – they handle human exchange. In reality, companies are nothing more than private planned economies. Man rather than money coordinates them. They are ruled by plans not price. Long-term contracts dominate at the expense of constant negotiations. The advent of hierarchical organisations meant that uncertainty could be artificially reduced. It worked. The efficiency gains were sometimes enormous.

In an information desert, companies rule. But now we are re-entering an information jungle where information is again available at our fingertips. We are back in the bazaar – though this time it resides in the virtual world, the Net neighbourhood.

Day by day, markets are becoming more efficient thanks to information technology. Markets are beginning to consume hierarchies – business firms and other organisations. Instead of making everything internally, companies have started buying more and more things from the external market. Instead of vertical integration

There is an on-demand revolution with the side effect of 'reversed queue phenomenon'. Companies, not customers, are waiting in line. Once you have opened up you can't close – if you snooze you lose.

– acquiring your suppliers and sometimes also your customers – the new trend is towards virtual integration and real disintegration.

Rather than one big, fat cat, there are now several mean, lean kittens working together in networks. Business-to-business e-commerce is currently five times bigger than consumer e-commerce. Business-to-business e-commerce is worth more than $4 trillion worldwide. By virtually linking up with other star-performers we can swap inventory for information. At Wal-Mart, the gigantic US retail chain, 97 per cent of goods never pass through a warehouse. The goods go directly from maker to shelf to you. The digital supply chain operates in real time. When you buy a woollen sweater from Benetton, the entire network feels it – all the way back to the sheep. A signal is sent from the cash register and, instantaneously, digital dominoes start falling. Soon, the entire network knows that it's time to produce a new sweater. All organisations are being forced to e-engineer their operations. They are turning their businesses into bazaars. Storage cost nil.

IT affects us all and affects everything. Your competitors are never more than a click away. Markets are consuming firms wherever you look. All organisations are now information based whether they are schools, the Red Cross, labour unions, the French Foreign Legion, rock groups or business firms.

Today it's the other way round. The mobile revolution is unwiring us all.

We are all becoming wired. The only difference is that some are good at using IT, while others are bad. Already, there are great geographical differences – not that long ago in the US there were 63 PCs per 100 workers – in Japan only 17.

A manager at a major construction company recently told us: 'The Internet is the best thing that has happened to the construction industry since the invention of the crane.' It enables a construction company to organise work in a totally new way. Indeed, as will be discussed later, IT enables and forces us all to reorganise and re-conceptualise our operations. In just a few years, the Internet has moved from being a solution looking for problems, to opening up the possibility of an entirely new business and societal logic. As sellers we can reach a larger market – the world is out there waiting in cyberspace. Not only that, distribution costs can be dramatically reduced by transferring bits rather than atoms. Just look at digital newspapers and computer games. As consumers, we can not only enjoy better prices and more convenience, but also a wider selection. If you were to print the cyberspace-based bookstore Amazon.com's product catalog it would be the size of 14 New York City phone books. In addition to convenience and lower prices, we can enjoy better service – instant feedback and advice on which items others with similar tastes have bought. In the end Amazon will not handle the products – only the information and the payment. (Try their Pro Merchant programme.)

We are in the process of moving from revolution to relevance. But, revolutions take time. Research carried out by Paul David at Stanford University shows that it took 20 years for factories to reap benefits from the introduction of the electric motor. As noted more than a century ago by economist Alfred Marshall: 'The full importance of an epoch-making idea is often not perceived in the generation in which it is made. A new discovery is seldom fully effective for practical purposes till many minor improvements and subsidiary discoveries have gathered themselves around it.' Change will not happen overnight. But it will happen. When? Professor Michael Hawley at MIT's Media Lab claims that 'When computing becomes as basic as Jockey shorts, as sexy as lingerie, as absorbent as Pampers we have arrived. Now we are there: YouTube, MySpace, SecondLife – the result will be big change.' We think we know what he means: it may take a little longer.

Still, one certainty is that 'infostructure', the electronic nervous system of the company, will become more important than infrastructure. Organisations with lousy 'infostructures' will look like 65-year-olds competing in the Olympic marathon wearing high heels and evening gowns.

FUNKY BUSINESS

INSTITUTIONS: REMAKING THE MAUSOLEUMS

The second driving force of change comes from institutions. Institutions are contractual arrangements, sets of agreements that bind people together within political parties, marriage, companies, nation states, families, supranational bodies and many other similar groupings. Institutions are the slumbering bedrock of our world. They are all the social structures that we humans create to promote stability and predictability. Institutions rest in large mausoleums as we busily go about our daily lives. They have a sense of timeless permanence. Untouched and apparently untouchable, they are there. And, because they are there, they matter.

Remember what we said earlier about the anonymous organisation of capitalism?

Traditionally, the role of institutions has been to simplify. Strong and stable institutions subsume our freedom. This reduces uncertainty. We are free, but within tidy parameters erected by our institutions. Institutions act as stabilisers, touches of grey to tone down the bright colours.

But though they look inert on the outside, institutions are continually developing. Institutions are changing in front of our eyes. They may appear to be sleeping giants but the moment our backs are turned they shift in their sleep, never to regain their previous posture.

Appearances can be deceptive. Confusingly, institutions often go out of their way to appear older than they actually are. Business schools, for instance, are institutions that like to give the impression of being older, and therefore more permanent, than they are in reality. A splash of ivy over the buildings is usually all it takes for them to convince themselves and everyone else they were there at the dawn of civilisation.

Institutions are not renowned for their creative, innovative or entrepreneurial abilities, but they are changing. They must.

Think of the pensioner surfers and hackers. And

Think of the pensioner surfers and hackers. And yet, paradoxically, the age of achievement has really turned into the age of appearance. Society is increasingly superficial. It used to be about what you did. Now, it is about how you appear. Paris Hilton is not famous for building a hotel chain; she is famous for being Paris Hilton.

In a wired world, where knowledge can easily be detached from people and places, competitiveness will depend upon having the best systems and institutional environments. Success will depend on having a fertile ground for developing and utilising knowledge; an environment in which ideas can be created, tried out, tinkered with, and exploited.

As new institutions develop, as there are what might be called institutional innovations, our lives are changed. The changes are not as obvious as when a bright new piece of technology impacts on our lives. Institutions do not – yet – come brashly branded in a box promising to halve our workload or weight.

But, think of the changes now happening within some of the major institutions that affect and influence our daily lives.

The Institution of Capitalism

At a macro level, institutional experiments abound. Communism, for example, was an institutional experiment that failed in the face of advancing technologies and changing values. Change did not come easily to societies built around five-year plans. Intellectual capital is difficult to explain and measure in a society in which capital is anathema.

After the fall of Communism, it would be easy to proclaim capitalism as the victor in the battle of institutional experiments. Celebration might be premature as there is now more than one type of capitalism. Indeed, there are *capitalisms*. The market economy comes in different dialects.

These dialects are based, somewhat vaguely at times, on the same principles. But they are assuredly different. Even the most apparently fixed institution is built on shifting sand.

First, we have the European version of social-liberal capitalism with a fairly strong state that can and will interfere. (Do what you want up to a point.) Then there is North American market capitalism with minimal intervention. (Do what you want.) A third type is the Far Eastern collective capitalism built on trust and a very strong state. (We all know what we are doing and so does the government.) A final version is the robber capitalism or *kleptocracy* that we currently find in a number of the former USSR countries and in some parts of Latin American. (Do what I want or I'll shoot you.)

Since we first wrote this we have seen Muhammad Yunus receive the Nobel Peace Price for his neo-bankerism. Give them a little of what they need and they will become capitalists.

At this point, you may indeed look around and conclude that capitalism's rude good health is a figment of our imagination. After all, recent years have seen a series of upheavals in major corporations with the downsizing demon wreaking havoc, as well as the Asian crisis and Russia's continuing problems in coming to terms with market forces. Then, there was Enron, Worldcom, Genoa, Seattle, Parmalat and all the rest.

We counter that capitalism is robust. Capitalism is not perfect but it's the least imperfect thing we have come up with so far. It will carry on. But the changes we are now seeing should not – and cannot – be underestimated. Capitalism is reinventing itself; carrying out a revolution from within. Revolutions are not over in a day or a night, they rumble on and on. It is like a movie with endless sequels. *Revolution* is followed by *Revolution II* then *Revolution III* ad infinitum. Unlike in the movie world, each has to outdo its predecessor. It is more like *Godfather* and *Godfather II*, one of the rare cases where the sequel actually outshone its predecessor, than *Rocky* and *Rocky II*.

The Nation State

In *Triad Power* (1985) Kenichi Ohmae argued that countries are mere governmental creations. In the emergent 'Interlinked Economy', envisaged by Ohmae, consumers are not driven to purchase things through nationalistic sentiments – no matter what politicians suggest or say. 'At the cash register,

Recall the gathering tsunami of cheap!

you don't care about country of origin or country of residence. You don't think about employment figures or trade deficits,' Ohmae wrote.

Ohmae is right. The nation state is no longer a relevant unit of analysis. The students who collect business school prospectuses from around the world aren't limited by or even concerned about nation states. Tomorrow's high achievers don't care if they study in Sweden, Italy, Germany, Taiwan, Argentina, Iceland, Australia, or South Africa. Their decision is made on the basis of what would be the best programme for them. No more and no less. They

Transparency is enabling a true meritocracy.

look at the usual stereotypical things – where are the best-looking girls and boys, the nicest beaches, the cheapest booze

Can the nation state help?

and the laziest classes? You may laugh, but remember that, with the exception of the last attribute, these may well be among the few factors that actually do provide the true sources of competitive advantage for a region in the future.

Multinational companies no longer think in terms of nation states. The furniture retailer IKEA will work with the best suppliers, wherever they may be. Why should you have a subsidiary in Finland, one in Norway and one in Sweden? Obviously, you have a Nordic office. Why should you have a subsidiary in Austria and one in Germany? You have a subsidiary for the German-speaking part of Europe or whatever. Other units of analysis – language, culture, age, climate, gender, lifestyle, sexual preferences, or whatever they may be – are more relevant.

The decline of the nation state is inextricably linked to the rise of internationalisation as a potent force in business and beyond. In institutional terms, we are going through a period of globalisation never before witnessed. For once, hype and reality are in accord. Whether it is through the European Union, the North American Free Trade Agreement or the Asian and Pacific Economic Cooperation, critical decisions are being transferred to a supranational level. We are building superstructures. Unfortunately there is not much evidence to suggest that superstructures are efficient. Maybe this explains why most modern business organisations are abandoning these solutions. The United Nations has long been a blunt instrument. The European Union is acting like an ambitious company of 20 or 30 years ago, wanting to do everything everywhere and, as a result, doing nothing very well.

From an economic perspective, the nation state is handing over the reins of power. We are living in a global economy. Today's markets are virtual and international rather than national. Information knows no boundaries. At a macro level, the critical problems and opportunities facing mankind can no longer be fruitfully defined as local ones. Unemployment is not a Dutch problem, nor a French problem; environmental pollution is not simply a German or a Turkish challenge. National efforts in such areas are commendable but they are, by their very nature, simply Band-Aids when radical surgery is required.

For such global issues, the nation state is far too small a unit for useful decision making. Unemployment, pollution, poverty and other such issues demand larger bodies able to make bigger decisions.

Then paradox kicks in. At the same time as the nation state is too small a unit, it is also, in other circumstances, too big. Increasingly, the nation state seems unable – sometimes unwilling – to help us with our small problems. What about my children's school? What about healthcare for my grandmother? Can the nation state help me? The nation state appears caught in the middle: too small to make an impact on the big issues; too big to make an impact on the small issues.

Political Parties

Political parties used to be institutions built on ideals. Most modern parties, from left to right, started as single-question groups with the aim of changing the world. Over time they evolved into opinion-conglomerates with a view on healthcare, the school system, law enforcement, pension systems, military service, etc. The trouble is that people are no longer coherent in their views. It might be more useful if we all had 10 votes to distribute between a number of parties, as they all have good *and* bad ideas. The attempts at unwieldy political coherence are out of step with our fragmented and incoherent perceptions and experiences of the world. As a result, the opinion-conglomerates are losing legitimacy and gaining only contempt and disdain. In the UK, more people voted before the last episode of *Big Brother* on TV than in one of the latest elections to the European Parliament. It may actually be deceptively simple to increase people's interest in politics. Instead of voting people into parliament, let's vote them out.

Not only that. Traditional political parties are also trapped in a geographical world. They are nationally structured. But, in a global world, who can take decisions that affect international capital markets, multinational firms and global super-specialists? Maybe, instead of hoping that the European Union or the United Nations can take care of all the global issues, and that any lack of global leadership should be handled by giving these institutions more power, we need to rethink our solutions more fundamentally. Perhaps, a more viable alternative is to establish a United Corporations. After all, the UN was set up at a time when the nation state was still a powerful and relevant unit of analysis. Today, companies rule the world, and this needs to be reflected in the institutions created to exert influence and control them.

The new political institutions are issue and problem based, and they are global. They are organisations like Greenpeace and Amnesty International. The trouble for them comes when they seek to make the leap to mainstream acceptance – the Green Party in Germany has, for example, struggled to become a multi-issue party. Instead of being efficient external provocateurs, they find themselves having to adapt and ending up as toothless and impotent. As Sir Winston Churchill pointed out: 'First we shape our structures – then our structures shape us.'

The Eternal Enterprise

The bureaucratic firm is dead. It is just too small for effective exploitation and too big for energetic experimentation. As we shall see later (see Funky Inc.), the corporation is, and has to be, reshaped along entirely new lines. 'Many companies need to reinvent themselves. And reinvention is not changing what is, but creating what isn't. A butterfly is not more of a caterpillar or a better or improved caterpillar; a butterfly is a different creature. Reinvention entails a series of continuous metamorphoses of this magnitude over time,' says American consultant and academic Richard Pascale.

At the heart of this reinvention is the realisation that companies should not and need not be around forever. In the past, corporate success was measured, as much as anything, by the ability to survive.

There are many 80-year-old people who have had tedious, unproductive lives and many people who die young after lives packed with excitement and achievement. Much the same happens with companies. The prevailing view has been that permanence is good. This explains why companies build such vast headquarters buildings. The bigger the better; the deeper the foundations and the higher the tower, the better the business. In this world, the size of the company's atrium is important. Atrium-envy is the rule.

Atrium-envy

Longevity is attractive because it is better than dying. This is a tidy, but not very persuasive argument. Yet, still faith is placed in companies lasting a long time. If they are around for a while, surely they must do some good. Arie de Geus in *The Living Company* quotes a Dutch survey of corporate life expectancy in Japan and Europe which came up with 12.5 years as the average life expectancy of all firms. 'The average life expectancy of a multinational corporation – *Fortune 500* or its equivalent – is between 40 and 50 years,' says de Geus, noting that one-third of 1970's *Fortune 500* companies had disappeared by 1983. Such mortality is attributed by de Geus to the focus of managers on profits and the bottom line rather than the human community which makes up their organisation. Fix this, and you have discovered the fountain of youth.

Time and time again, research suggests that companies fail to last the course. W. Chan Kim and Renée Maubourgne's bestseller, *Blue Ocean Strategy*, pointed out that entire sectors disappear. In his book, *Sweet Spot*, the marketer Arun Sinha says: 'According to the experts, half of all S&P 500 will not be around by the year 2020. The consulting firm McKinsey & Company went back to 1935 and tracked all the S&P 500 companies since then and found out that half of them disappear every 20 years.'

But what if de Geus is absolutely wrong in suggesting that firms should aspire to live forever? Greatness is fleeting and, for corporations, it will become ever more fleeting. The ultimate aim of a business organisation, an artist, an athlete or a stockbroker may be to explode in a dramatic frenzy of value creation during a short space of time rather than to live forever. Somewhat surprisingly, the places with the highest growth rates and most dramatic success stories, such as Silicon Valley and the Houston IT-cluster, also have an extremely high rate of corporate mortality.

For firms, this implies that the company becomes more disposable – a temporary camp for nomadic individuals who then move on to meet new people and challenges. After all, we have a disposable mind-set in virtually every other area of life. Maybe we should, in the words of Sir Paul McCartney, 'Live and let die'.

The disposable company is not a new phenomenon. Among the first enterprises we know of are the ancient vessels that sailed from upper to lower Egypt to collect gold, diamonds and slaves. People invested in such ships and, if and when they returned, the investors and the crew struck gold. After the journey, this specific enterprise was terminated. History repeats itself. So, don't be surprised if in the future it proves much more rewarding to be a reincarnating insect than a 300-year old-tortoise. The firm with a future, shortlived or not, is energetic rather than eternal. Listen to Canadian rock legend Neil Young: 'It's better to burn out than to fade away.'

> **Of course, against all expectations Neil Young has turned out to be a great survivor. His work and the channels for his work have evolved with technology and with time. Hats off to Neil.**

The Family

There is a mystical aura around the concept of family, a rosy glow of well-being. The family is the maternal bosom. It is the sugary sentimentality of *The Waltons*. It is mother and father standing proudly with their children. It is well balanced and sophisticated; warm and uncomplicated; unsullied by reality.

Of course, domestic reality is quite different from the saccharined sentiments served up by the advertising and media industries. No matter how bright, happy and sophisticated their members may be, families are all dysfunctional. It is simply a question of how dysfunctional.

There is little doubt that traditional notions of what constitutes a family are breaking down. Divorce rates are skyrocketing and a lot of young people never marry or marry extremely late in life – they stay single or just live together. Dinkies rule. As it stands, the family could soon become a luxury item – happily married couples with 2.4 happy children (a pet dog, and a whitewashed house with a wicker fence) will be the exceptions, unusual archetypes of a fading ideal. Although laws and regulations do not always reflect it, for many the de facto standard is already serial monogamy, threesomes, etc. Lots of kids are brought up without being exposed to long-lasting, permanent relationships. They may have two fathers and three mothers. Two of their brothers have another dad, and their sisters have a totally different set of parents. And then we expect them to work for one company and one boss for the rest of their lives!

And if people indeed form families, they no longer spend that much time together. During the 1960s, US fathers on average talked some 45 minutes per day with their kids. Today, the equivalent figure is six minutes.

We are brought up with a set of notions. Previous generations called them standards and are fond of telling younger generations that standards have fallen. The reality is that standards have changed. Yet, when it comes to families we are still measured against previous family values. We consider ourselves to be failures. There is a nagging suspicion that we are aiming unreasonably high. Perhaps there is nothing wrong. We are just different.

VALUES: FROM TELESCOPES TO KALEIDOSCOPES

The final part of the triad of driving forces is value systems. For better or worse, values affect all of our thoughts and deeds. Values are the way we relate to work, technologies and people. Values influence artefacts and actions. Values are enormously powerful, omnipresent and hugely different from place to place, person to person. Values create unity and conflicts. But values also change – slowly, very slowly.

Working Values

Capitalism and Christianity are close relations. We would never have seen capitalism, as we know it, without the Protestant revolution resulting in a new work ethic. Martin

Luther said that we should pray and work – *ora et labora* in Latin. Work in itself was good, an act of homage, spirit enhancing and humbling.

The corollary of this is that the actual nature of the work is not that important. Work is good. And, if you spend 12 hours working on a machine carrying out repetitive tasks, work is still good. The act of work is good; therefore, you want to and need to work. Luther's edict produced generation upon generation of self-motivated workers. They wanted to work because work was the route to betterment.

Look elsewhere and value systems are at odds with basic Western conceptions. While work was the fulcrum of the Western world – and the basis of our initial industrial pre-eminence – the East embraced its own Luther: Confucius. Luther venerated work; Confucius venerated wisdom. In the Far East, many people start to save money for their children's education before they have even found a partner. In the East wisdom is all.

In Eastern economies many people believe in both Buddha and Confucius. Buddhism stands for horizontal solidarity and Confucianism propagates vertical subordination. What for most Westerners is a classical oxymoron and paradox – being simultaneously horizontal and vertical – is for these people the most natural thing in the world. Add capitalism to create a little direction, and you get a mean machine moving at the speed of light. Put Communism on top of this system, and you get another type of mean machine – there are far too many who can verify that particular fact.

Values differ. The Chinese economy is built on the concept of trust – *Guanxi* – a strong and inexpensive substitute for contracts and lawyers. This concept extends to the overseas Chinese who tend to cooperate wherever they are. They have created a global network in which knowledge and capital, goods and services flow freely. How much business would you do in the absence of contracts? If it came down to trust, how many colleagues, suppliers and customers would you really get involved with?

Values differ. In Japan, robots are named after famous singers. How many of you have an ABB Madonna at your job? A Japanese union's idea of a strike is a one-hour work stoppage timed for the lunch break. Since the firm is the family, the goals of employee and employer overlap. A strike during working hours would, therefore, be counter-productive – you would effectively be striking against yourself.

Muhammad Yunus in *Banker to the Poor* points out that, in banking parlance 'credit' really means trust. Yet, banks seem to show little trust when they ask you to mortgage all you have so that you can be credit worthy. Values differ.

Fusion in the Global Village

Now, values have been geographically liberated. Value systems were once local. In our part of the world, the church was in the middle of the village and had a monopoly over local values. Now, next door to the church you are liable to find a mosque. Back in 1970, some 10,000 Muslims lived in our home country. Today, there are more than 350,000. We are continually exposed to different values. Assumptions have been replaced by a need for decisions. We have to choose. Do we visit the church or the mosque? What is the difference between the values of the two? This is the MeWe generation.

Often the end result is not as clear-cut as it once was. Now we might believe in God while embracing other cultures and other values. The actor Richard Gere proclaims his Buddhist beliefs while at the same time carrying on a successful career in the distinctly non-Buddhist surroundings of Los Angeles. We are internally consistent but, to the institutions and values outside, a bewildering juxtaposition.

The new reality is reflected in the make-up of management teams; football teams; what we buy; what we eat – Thai chicken wings (Buffalo-style) with pasta; how we live; and who we are. Cultures, tastes, experiences collide to create a cornucopia of values. Bollywood meets hip-hop with a touch of Sinatra. Mongrel mania.

Fusion is too easily identified with confusion. The two do not necessarily follow. Japanese philosophies can operate successfully with Western philosophies. American companies can succeed in Japan. But success will only come to those who appreciate and are sensitive to different value systems. Competition is now global and value based.

Labradoodle

As values have been recombined in powerful fusions and moved beyond national boundaries, old assumptions have been tossed aside. There are no easy and generally held answers to questions about the value of material possessions versus knowledge, about right and wrong, good and evil. The questions remain,

Even evident among canines where dog combos have been legitimised – think of the labradoodle, a barking-glad combo of labrador and poodle.

but the answers have become more blurred. For the first time in history, people from various parts of the world with partly different definitions of what constitutes what Socrates once called a 'good life' are going to compete. Individualists against collectivists. Uncertainty reducers against uncertainty producers. All against all.

Spiritual Emptiness

Behind all these effects we see a gigantic spiritual vacuum. The meaning of life has given way to the meaning of lite. It is a mist sweeping over the world filling us with doubts and hesitation. We are no longer pilgrims with a clear mission living in a well-structured environment. Instead, we have become wandering vagabonds in search of who knows what.

This trend is especially noticeable in a country such as Sweden. Its Welfare State and social systems were supposed to be the best in the world, and yet country after country now appears to be passing Sweden by. Perhaps it is time to start questioning the basic beliefs and to determine what values are still viable in a borderless information society. Close friends are more important to 18-year-old Scandinavians than their families or school teachers.

Is this the end of religion? Do the Ten Commandments, Sharia or Bahá'í belong to the group of endangered species? How many of your friends regularly go to church and really believe in something other than themselves? French author Émile Zola was right back in 1886 when he observed: 'We have stopped believing in God, but not in our own immortality.' Is this the end of ideologies? No wonder that only half of the voters exercised their right to elect the new president of the US, 'the world's greatest democracy', back in 1996. The figures for 2004 weren't much better – 60.3 per cent – and that's on the back of a divisive war. In the 1999 election to the European Parliament, in many nations less than 40 per cent of the citizens voted. Democracy turns demo*crazy*. When people are loyal only to themselves, or whatever may be the worthy cause of the month, can we talk about the end of solidarity? We live in a world in which we buy letters of indulgence by watching Live8, sending a few bucks to Greenpeace or wearing a red nose for Comic Relief.

Is this the end of the modern project? Have we given up the idea of building a society in which all people can prosper? Hasn't the acceptance of leaving a few lost souls out in the gutter risen during the past few years? And without soul, objectives, and meaning, is this not the end of progress? After all, if you have no idea of where you want to end up, it does not really matter which road you take.

Pope Paul VI foresaw this development some 35 years ago. He rightly claimed that, 'Technological society has succeeded in multiplying the opportunities for pleasure, but it has great difficulty in generating joy.' So, welcome to a world of violence, sex, drugs and rock'n'roll. A global freak-show. Jerry Springer-ville.

DEREGULATING LIFE: CONDEMNED TO FREEDOM

The three drivers of technology, institutions and values have created an international, knowledge-based world. In this new environment competition is total, personal and generic. If knowledge is key we are all competing against each other. The genie is out of the bottle and cannot be replaced. People who spend their time putting genies back into bottles should not be approached, let alone employed. There is no going back. While a great many people recognise the genie is out, few have sufficient insight to turn this recognition into action.

Freedom has been thrust back into our hands. Institutions used to work to create certainty. Now, the certainties are withering. Blind loyalty has died. We no longer proclaim lifelong loyalty to institutions no matter what they are or what they do. We shop around. Lifelong membership is defunct, whether it be of a political party, a relationship, a fan club, a company or a country. We are more promiscuous about our institutions. Promiscuity is based on choice. Technology used to be concerned with mechanisation. Now, it creates complex systems. Values used to be built around strictures and clear expectations. Now, values are a moveable feast as our value systems are liberalised.

We are deregulating the banking industry, the telecoms industry, the airline industry, the energy industry, etc. We are deregulating morally. We are deregulating technologically. As individuals, we could cross any boundary – gender included. Indeed, we are deregulating life for ourselves and for our children. They can freely choose where to live, what to do, where to work, what to study and who to be. They can choose to be homosexual, heterosexual, sadomasochistic or transvestites. They can choose when to work and when they want children, if they want children at all. We have the power of choice. It is the American dream to the max – total freedom.

Enjoy it. Tomorrow we are going to wake up in a world in which we all need to realise that we are condemned to freedom – the freedom to choose. There is no escape. Institutions won't shoulder responsibility because they are in a state of confused flux. There is no church, no village, no town, no nation state, no market to rely on. There are no cut-and-dried values to use as escape tools. Technology exists to create opportunities, to create efficiency, not to take responsibility from us. So, we are faced with the prospect of taking charge of our own freedom.

With choice comes responsibility. Responsibility for our own health, for our own education, for our own careers – responsibility for our own lives. The more opportunities there are, the more responsibilities there are for us as individuals.

We have been given greater responsibility at a time when the old certainties have evaporated. The institutions, values and technologies that previously existed are disappearing. The decisions and choices of today and the future will be made in a climate of all-embracing uncertainty.

Coping with Chaos

Chaotic times are here again. The trouble is that the human race does not react very well to uncertainty. Change inevitably leads to unrest. One generic response to this is to reduce freedom dramatically. The fascist movements of the twentieth century emerged from periods of economic turmoil and uncertainty. People cried out for strong leaders – leaders who could reduce uncertainty. Today, the uncertain are as likely to join a religious sect as a political party. People join because

The Welfare Society appears to be designed by IKEA – it comes in self-assembly flat packs without assembly instructions.

the complexity and uncertainty of everyday life can be removed. They don't have to worry about income tax, office politics or their credit cards. They surrender doubt with certainty. True believers have, it is often said, a faraway look in their eyes. For true believers this is literally true. They have opted out. The downside is that you always have to opt in to something – and if that something eliminates uncertainty and doubt it is probably not good for your long-term mental health.

While a minority cope with uncertainty by disappearing into the distance, muttering mantras and following their leader, others switch on the TV. TV convinces you that things could be worse. This, sadly, explains the rise of freak show TV as exemplified by the Jerry Springer show. The show succeeds because it makes viewers feel normal. Even Dr Phil and the super nannies make us feel superior. We watch TV to figure out ourselves, to be reassured that we're better off, mentally, physically or financially, then the freaks on display.

Avoiding uncertainty is human nature. Companies bring in consultants to buy uncertainty reduction. We can't figure out what is happening so let's bring in some people who are really bright and have a model to deal with this sort of thing. The consultant's report is nothing more than a corporate comforter. We know of a consultant who offers his clients three choices: Do you want corporate Valium, a boardroom alibi or business results, he asks.

Throughout the business world there are a profusion of models, frameworks and assumptions. All are managerial versions of Prozac: guaranteed uncertainty reducers. Managers – hardly a breed associated with revolution – have created their own messiahs and their own religious sects in management gurus. The latest acronyms have been guaranteed to give the CEOs a good night's sleep and people months of meaningless reorganisation. Try TQM and now BPR and then master JIT.

Uncertainty reduction is a ritualistic part of corporate life. When you start a job, you spend a day or two on an induction programme. The organisation tells you how to behave. It is dressed up in nice, friendly corporate language, but that is

True leaders set people free

basically what is happening. We believe that such complacent corporate certainty now has to give way to complexity. We believe that the optimum response must be to embrace complexity – not try to eliminate it. Complexity is horrific but fascinating. We have to have the courage to face it.

It may save our sanity. After all, if you measure yourself against uncertainty, life tends to look a little better. In contrast, measuring yourself against certainty is irrelevant and depressing. If everything is in a state of flux the only fixed thing is the individual. A defined picture of yourself is as much as you can hope for.

In the recent past our roles were pre-defined. The church, the family or the corporation provided the historical script. No more. To be successful in a world of improvisational theatre, you have to ask yourself questions. You have to know yourself and your objectives. It is Management by Objectives for individuals. Defining yourself is the only means of creating a good life. This gives leaders, anywhere in organisations, a new job. They must produce uncertainty. Real leaders challenge people. They do not control them. True leaders set people free.

3

FUNKY

'The more the merrier' Proverb

We are so small and there is so much of everything. Look up at the stars and count. Look down from a plane and contemplate the lights. We are insignificant, overwhelmed by the seas of choice and the tides of change. There is so much. The trouble is, like Oliver Twist, we keep asking for more.

We want to bungee jump. Then we want to bungee over a canyon. Then from a helicopter. Then naked. Then naked while whistling Neil Diamond's greatest hits.

This is the age of more. More choice. More consumption. More fun. More fear. More uncertainty. More competition. More opportunities. We have entered a world of excess: an age of abundance.

It is a shock. Think back to the pictures of Moscow's premier department store, GUM that you would see on the TV news in the seventies and eighties . The shelves were always

The fall doesn't take long.

completely – and somewhat comically if you lived in the West – empty. A rotund Russian stood at a bare counter. Behind him there was always a single bottle of extra-strength diesel fuel masquerading as vodka. The lonely Muscovite housewife lingered by the empty shelves dreaming of excess in a world of constraint.

That was then. This is now: think Saks Fifth Avenue, eBay, Printemps, Selfridges, Amazon.com, Macy's, Gallerie Lafayette, Harrods or Zara. Even in Moscow, bare shelves have been replaced by glorious excess. For bread and circuses read champagne and caviar, canapés and trinkets. Visit the upmarket ski resort of Courchevel and you will see Russians arriving at the snowy landing strip in their private planes and then gorging themselves on the most expensive champagne and exorbitantly priced food. Welcome to canapé capitalism. If you wish to travel to Karlo Vivary (former Karlsbad) in the Czech Republic for a spa holiday you'd better book months in advance. The massage tables are laden with Russian ladies who need to get their extra canapé kilos smoothed.

THE SURPLUS SOCIETY

In Norway – population 4.6 million – you can choose from 200 different newspapers, 100 weekly magazines and some 20 TV channels. In Sweden – population 9 million – the number of beers to choose from has increased from around 50 to over 350 in little more than 10 years. A single year can see the publication of 1,700-plus business books in the American market. Major label record companies launched 30,000 albums in the US in one year. In the same country, the number of annual grocery product launches has increased from 2,700 to some 20,000. To keep up with all the product launches, Procter & Gamble has more scientists on its payroll (over 7,000) than Harvard, Berkeley and MIT combined. There are more than 10 million blogs on the Internet and 40,000 new ones are added every day.

Profusion abounds. The lady in GUM now has over 50 channels on NTV-Plus, the first and the only direct-to-home

An interesting side issue to this is how P&G has recalibrated its R&D efforts. Instead of getting great ideas from the inside and taking them to market, the company now focuses on working with external people to come up with tomorrow's products. Called Connect & Develop, its new approach to R&D is reaping dividends.

More of the same?

satellite TV system in Russia, and a quarter of a billion home pages to choose from (though the supermarket remains devoid of anything she can afford). Viva choice! Seiko turns out more than 5,000 separate watch models. In one year, Sony launched 5,000 new products – more than two new products per working hour. Maybe this is necessary in a market where the average product life cycle for consumer electronics products is now three months. Still, compared to Walt Disney, Sony's innovation record is nondescript. Former Disney CEO Michael Eisner once claimed that the company develops a new product – a film, a comic book, a CD, or whatever – every five minutes.

Excess is in and the route to this world of excess is the TV. The temple of our times is not the church, but the TV. The battle for our souls is acted out every weekday night as David Letterman, king of American late-night TV, fights it out with Jay Leno to capture the interest of the average John and Jane Doe of the US TV audience. The concept is simple: 10 minutes of talk followed by a commercial; then more talk and a commercial; more talk, more commercials. At the end of the day, the average American citizen has been exposed to some 247 ads. By the time they reach the age of 18, they have encountered 350,000 TV commercials. And now we have the Internet live on TV, fully interactive TV. Press the red button, now! We have digital everything and your living room is getting very crowded indeed.

And knowledge, too, is exploding. Think of the 100,000-plus IT engineers developing software in Bangalore – their numbers gaining fast on Silicon Valley. Think of the profusion of MBA graduates. Think of the leap in numbers of people going through college. Think of the flood of scientists. Think of the well-educated Desert Storm soldiers. K Club is not only a golf course.

The world is alive with knowledge, with products and services, with information. But more often simply means more of the same. The surplus society has a surplus of similar companies, employing similar people, with similar educational backgrounds, working in similar jobs, coming up with similar ideas, producing similar things, with similar prices, warranties and qualities. And even though they may not yet know it, all these firms, individuals and customer offerings are competing. It is karaoke capitalism and there's always someone wanting the mic. This is good news if you are a customer; and time for prayer if you are an executive.

Three key forces lie behind the emergence of the surplus society: the growth in markets resulting in market mania; senseless oversupply; and technological advances which have made communication more or less costless. And behind these forces, we can again discern the influence of changes in technology, institutions and values.

Market Mania

The first element in creating this world of excess is the growth in markets. There are now more markets for more things, covering a larger geographical area than ever before. Deregulation and trade liberalisation have unleashed market forces on virtually every human activity. At the turn of the twentieth century, some 10–15 per cent of the world population lived within a market system. In the 1970s, approximately 40 per cent of all individuals lived within such a system. Today, we are talking about 90 per cent or more.

But not all markets are global yet. Take labour markets. Only 1.5 per cent of the labour force works outside its home country. In the European Union (462 million people and growing), the equivalent number is 2 per cent. Capital still flows more freely than people.

The International Labor Organisation (ILO) estimates there are 20 million migrant workers, immigrants and members of their families across Africa; 18 million in North America; 12 million in Central and South America; 7 million in South and East Asia; 9 million in the Middle East; and 30 million across all of Europe. That's a lot of people.

Still, in this crazy world there are markets for absolutely everything. Markets in commodities and capital; body parts; every conceivable type of sex; any industrial component you can think of; and any kind of service you can imagine. There are markets in betting – spread betting applies the logic of the futures exchange to sporting bets; markets in alcohol – a Dutch nightclub entrepreneur operates a futures market in drinks at his clubs; and markets in knowledge and talent. Imagine markets in body decoration or markets in museums.

Feel the funk. If you want to – and can afford to – you can even hire Versailles to throw the ultimate office party. Some 200 years after the French revolution, the Hall of Battles is yours for a mere $70,000. Or why not choose somewhere a bit further afield, a little different – like the American investment bank which partied in the Forbidden City in the People's Republic of China. Everything has a price. The Louvre is on the market to Abu Dhabi. Markets rule.

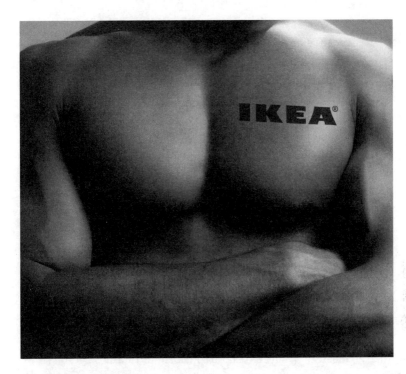

Senseless Supply

In the recent past the world was a big place. Cutting-edge technological knowledge was to be found in the industrialised Western world. That was where the renowned universities, aggressive companies and other competence-producing organisations were based. This was the age before the joint venture and the strategic alliance; before collaboration was made easy through technology; before the explosion of new, different technologies.

In this world, demand mostly exceeded supply. After the Second World War, there was a great surge for new jobs, products and services. The European and Asian industrial infrastructures were in ruins. This was great news for any company in any industry. We were at their mercy – as employees and consumers. Moreover, the rate of technological change and proliferation of customer preferences was not as great as it now is. Things moved slowly and usually moved locally. This was the world of mass production where markets were assumed and taken for granted; where customers were told what they wanted – every colour so long as it was black. Weighed down with managerial layers and with no apparent need to broaden perspectives, companies sailed on like supertankers on autopilot.

The rocks are here and the lighthouse has closed down. In industry after industry, and in market after market, supply is beginning to exceed demand. Business professors Sumantra Ghoshal and Christopher Bartlett noted: 'In the slow-growth 1990s, however, overcapacity is the norm in most businesses: 40 per cent in automobiles, 100 per cent in bulk chemicals, 50 per cent in steel, and 140 per cent in computers, for example. Both technological progress and customer needs are driving toward smaller lot sizes and higher variety.' Slow growth lingers like a bad smell in many Western economies.

Old local companies can, and do, now compete all over the world. New companies can, and do, now enter traditional industries. Think of Lenovo's acquisition of IBM's personal computing business or Dong Feng's entry into Europe. As firms no longer need to make everything that they plan to sell – they can buy it from someone else – entry barriers are evaporating. Totally new entrants, or firms that historically competed in other industries, can combine components from other companies. They don't need huge amounts of capital or specialist knowledge. Invisible invaders can attack conventional companies from all directions. Supply is surging – and it will keep on surging.

Costless Communication

Finally comes the phenomenon of decreased communication costs. Information costs have dramatically plummeted. In 1930, a three-minute call from New York to London cost some $250 (in 1990 dollars). Thirty years later, the cost for a similar phone call was down to $50. Now, we are approaching zero. Indeed, Skype-to-Skype calls are just that. Similarly, the cost of sending a 40-page document from LA to Washington is $9 by fax; $16 by FedEx; $3 by snail-mail; and 9 cents by email. The Internet provides zero-variable-transaction-costs – costs that occur when you do business (setting up and controlling contracts, etc.). Little wonder that Michael Dell has said that the Internet is surpassed only by telepathy.

Sending information has never been cheaper. Ditto searching for information. IT enables us to scan the entire market. We can scan the world. Armed with our search engines, we are no longer restricted to the special offers in our neighbourhood. Just Google it! The flood of information allows us always to find the best deal. Infomediaries are already a powerful force. Some 16 per cent of all US car buyers shop online before turning up at a dealer. The Internet, or any other source of processed information, makes comparison shopping a picnic.

The Return of the Demanding Customer

We are moving towards increasingly perfected markets. The result is total competition. In the surplus society the customer is more than a king: the customer is the mother of all dictators. And this time it's for real. If the customer speaks you have to jump high and jump fast. The customer wants products in orange with purple spots. The customer wants them today in Fiji. You have to deliver otherwise you will soon be out of business. As Lou Gerstner, former

Witness IBM's innovation jams which involve employees and customers in live and vibrant debate about great ideas. The town hall meeting just came of age.

chairman and CEO of IBM, put it: 'Control... has been tacitly transferred into the hands of tens of millions – soon hundreds of millions – of users worldwide.' Power to the people. Over the past 40 years the consumer has gone from cheeping mouse to roaring lion; from nice, stupid and humble to mean, smart and demanding.

This is only the beginning. People now use the Net to link up with their binary siblings – other individuals with similar

Roaring lion?

cravings. They will join hands and create unions – customer
unions. If you are buying a new car, how much bargaining
power do you have in relation to Ford Motors, Honda,
DaimlerChrysler, or even the smallest car company in the world?
Not a lot. But, what if you could link up with 999 other consumers
who are interested in

**Customers rule. Try employing
your customers and get them
to pay you for working for you
– witness the business model
of eBay and others.**

buying the same car? Today, we can. The power is ours to use
and abuse. Consumers of the world unite. Technology provides
the tools. Values provide the frame.

Some may assert that they're unlikely to see any of these
developments in their industry. Maybe they won't, but, one way
or another, we will all be affected. There will be no exceptions.
Your suppliers may be directly affected, or your customers. If
so, so will you. The force of the demanding customer or client

will be felt up and down the supply chain. Universities will feel it. Soul singers will feel it. Car companies will feel it. Diamond dealers will feel it – if they survive the attack from the 2007 movie *Blood Diamonds.* The question of who will pay for this is not clear – maybe all firms will. The question of who will be the ultimate winner is easier – the final customer: you. We own the marketplace, lock, stock and barrel.

Competing for Attention

In an age of abundance, companies have to work hard to get noticed. They are on constant tip-toe at the back of the frame trying to squeeze in. Companies are competing for a few seconds of attention. They want to be noticed in the tidal wave of information hitting everyone, everywhere, and all the time. In fact, they have to be noticed.

To get noticed, they go to extremes. Excess is a business necessity. In a commercial for Miller's beer a magician makes hair grow from the armpits of the women around him. A Mercedes Benz TV commercial in the United States features a woman who so enjoys driving the car that 20 seconds into the spot she has an orgasm – from driving a car. Extreme times call for extreme measures. This is a seen it, had it, heard it, done it, been there type of society. Sameness sucks!

In the funky village, real competition no longer revolves around market share. We are competing for attention – *mindshare and heart share*. If you cannot capture the attention of prospective customers or employees, you are out. To attract them, you need to provide experiences that are immediate, intense and instant. In an excess economy, attention is scarce. Handle it with care.

Indeed, we may well have to start paying for attention. American marketing star Seth Godin talked about permission marketing. In many countries legislators have now forbidden spam marketing.

Seth Godin is now a few marketing ideas and books on from permission marketing. Check out http://sethgodin.typepad.com.

Our contacts with those customers who don't want to drown in a tidal wave of information will be by invitation only. Yesterday, we had to pay for newspapers, phone calls and Internet connections. Today, we can get them for free, as long as we are prepared to read, listen to or watch ads. Tomorrow, we will be paid for it. You Tube has announced they will pay for your contribution of home movies to their site. We will be paid to receive a particular newspaper, to use a particular telephone company or Internet service provider. Paying for attention is the logical progression of what is already happening.

Not only is the funky village marked by abundance and excess, the three driving forces also cause dramatic changes in time, mass and space. Everything is being turned upside down and inside out. We used to do business in a world where there was plenty of time; what mattered could be seen and touched; and the game was taking place in our own backyard. No more. Now, a weird wired world is unravelling in front of our eyes. The new society is developing in real time; competition is brain based; and the economy is globally linked.

Let us provide you with a road map for the future. The current contraction in time and expansion in space leave you standing here.

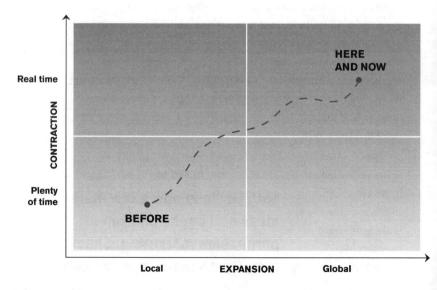

NOW: THE REAL-TIME SOCIETY

Time is the new religion of our age. We are addicted to speed. The new society operates in real time. What once used to take three years, then took three months, then three days, then three hours, and then three minutes, now takes three seconds – approaching zero. In the real-time economy prices are set second by second; companies compete on how fast they can be to develop, make and launch products. In the real-time world we live live. This is the CNN society, instantly linked by satellite to where the action is. It is a remote-control reality. If you cannot arouse my interest; if you don't appeal to my values; I will zap to someone else who can. We have to do business MTV-style. Or else, zap – or even, click! The most staggering thing is that, in such a world, companies keep on publishing *Annual Reports*! We admire their persistence, but shake our heads at their resistance.

The new heroes are *staminacs* – people who never seem to sleep. Bill Gates, who claims to relax quite a bit nowadays, said that: 'There are days that I work fourteen hours, but most days I don't work more than twelve hours. On weekends I rarely work more than eight hours.' Bill is

A combo of fun and fear drive modern knowledge workers to put in 80-hour weeks. We no longer work out of moral obligation. Since the advent of computers, we all come with an expiry date. We could be obsolete tomorrow. Little wonder we work and work and work and work.

not alone. Between 1970 and 2002 the average number of hours worked in the United States increased by 20 per cent. It is not only Bill Gates who works unfeasibly and unhealthily long hours. We all really should get out more.

While working harder is one natural response to the funky world we find ourselves in, we seriously doubt that it is the best answer. If it were, the ultimate winners in the funky village would be people with little or no need to sleep. Instead of working harder, funky people work smarter. They do what they are really good at, maybe 100 times better. Period. Try beating that by reducing sleep.

Grow or I will zap

Advances in technology have pushed us into a totally and funkily connected economy. And connected systems allow for real-time feedback. The dominant organisation of the past may legally have been one entity, but was often better characterised as disconnected or even dismembered. It could take four weeks, or maybe sometimes four months, for the factory to hear from the sales people at the other end of the world about booms or slumps. In the wired world supply-chain feedback is instant. When something happens in Milan, the partners in New York, Montevideo and Sydney know about it immediately. Think Benetton; think sheep.

Firms, supply chains, industries, markets and even entire economies are being transformed into ultra-sensitive systems where changes anywhere are instantly registered everywhere. It's like pulling in fishing net – no matter where you start pulling, kinetic energy will be reproduced throughout the entire net. It's like a cobweb where the spider is capable of sensing movement wherever a bug or fly has landed in the web. But remember that such sensitive systems are fragile. Every now and then they can, and do, break down or collapse.

Why, then, is real-time feedback so important? Let us provide just a few examples. Currently, in the computer industry, component costs decline by approximately one per cent every week. You don't want inventory – you want instant information. As noted earlier, the key to success is substituting information for inventory. In the first edition of *Funky Business* we noted that Dell turns around its inventory 52 times per year. The equivalent number for Compaq is 13.5 and for IBM it's 9.8. Our latest figures are that Dell turned its inventory 107 times per year – an astounding advantage over HP and IBM, which flipped their inventories 8.5 and 17.5 times per year, respectively. In which company would you buy stocks? Indeed, IBM later suffered the consequences and divested its entire PC division to Chinese competitor Lenovo.

In addition, real-time feedback enables organisations to respond much quicker and more accurately to customer demands. We can get better service. For instance, buying a bunch of CDs or books over the Net, we can immediately find out if they are in 'stock' (at least virtually). Information on the books or CDs which people with similar tastes have bought is at our fingertips. Reviews, written by other customers, on the items we are planning to buy are displayed on the screen in front of us. It's the return of the local grocery store, where the dealer always knew the special interests and demands of Mrs Jones or Mr Black, though this time in digital form. Scary or great service, or both. What is, is.

The Age of Auctions

The main impact of the real-time society on business is in making way for the age of auctions. In the bazaar, the fish market, or at a traditional auction, prices were (and still are) always set in real time. Over time, shifts in supply and demand determine the price. Financial markets still function in that way. When we buy stocks in Motorola, Apple, Sony, Nokia or Samsung, we do not know exactly how much we are paying until the deal is closed. But when we get a new mobile phone from any of these companies we know the price in advance. Why? The simple answer is that fixed prices reduce uncertainty, for both the seller and the buyer – Prozac pricing. In the funky village, however, change is a constant and instead of reducing uncertainty the emphasis will be on reducing friction – all the stuff that prevents the realisation of perfect markets. In an info desert, lack of information or asymmetrically distributed information – the seller knows things that the buyer does not have a clue about, like when you buy a used car – all prevent the realisation of market perfection. But in an info jungle, sooner or later, friction-free capitalism will happen.

Thanks to new technology and changes in our values, prices for any type of good or service can once more be set instantly – as a consequence of changes in supply and demand. Think of Ryanair, easyJet and an array of others. Everything is up for auction. This is precarious or variable pricing. We are back in the bazaar, but this time the bazaar is not necessarily limited in space. Back in 1999, online auctioneer eBay carried 9,000 products in 1,086 categories and had 140,000,000 hits per week. Now, eBay has 212 million members worldwide; 19 million items on its sites at any given time, more than 300 times the number of stock-keeping units of your average Wal-Mart store; and sells $20 billion plus worth of goods in a year.

Real-time pricing spreads like a forest fire. We see it in the power utility industry, electronics industry, telecoms industry and airline industry. But real-time pricing is not necessarily tied to the Internet. The principle goes far beyond that. Some of the vending machines that Coca-Cola distributes around the world are loaded with electronics as well as Coke. The technology enables the machine to sense the local conditions. Is it raining or is the sun shining? What is the temperature? Coca-Cola believes that local conditions are good indicators of what kind of demand there will be for a can of Coke. If the sun is shining a can may cost a dollar. If it is raining heavily, the price might go down to 50 cents.

So what are the consequences of precarious, variable pricing for us as consumers or business managers? Some ideas might be gleaned from markets with a lot of experience in operating real time. In financial markets, for example, you design your own risk level, cafeteria style, by using a range of instruments such as options. Let's say you are planning to buy

Prices are set in real time

a new motorbike. Prices are set in real time so you do not know in advance what you are going to pay. The bike you have been looking at is gaining in popularity so you fear that prices may go up. To handle the risk, you buy a bike-option that two months ahead will allow you to acquire the motorcycle for a fixed price. Sixty days later, three things may have happened. The bike may cost just as much as your set price plus the cost of the option, or it may cost more or less. But what really matters is that you had an instrument that helped to design your own risk profile. You may use it or not. You may minimise or maximise your exposure to risk. You decide because you are in charge. These arrangements have worked for years in the financial world, so why can't they work when we buy a motorbike, flat-screen TV or car?

SOFTWHERE: THE BRAIN-BASED SOCIETY

In the beginning there were products and services, things we made or things we delivered. Then money became the great bean-feast. In the 1980s doing imaginative things with money – derivatives, junk bonds, leveraged buyouts, futures – was the way to make it really big. Now, doing imaginative things with information is the road to riches. Walter Wriston, the former chairman of Citibank, was right: information about money is now more valuable than money itself. Of course money still matters. But the price of money is called real interest rate and it has steadily gone down.

Look at New York Mayor Michael Bloomberg. After running the investment bank Salomon Brothers' equity trading and technology systems, Bloomberg left the company in 1981. With a group of fellow ex-Salomon employees, Bloomberg founded Innovative Market Systems – later renamed Bloomberg. It now has annual revenues in excess of $4 billion and Bloomberg has departed to run New York. Bloomberg's insight was that though he was successful trading with money, he could make even more when he reported on money and gave people information about money.

In the information age, information is dollars. Matt Drudge is the man at the keyboards in his LA office controlling the *Drudge Report*. He styles himself as a kind of Woodward and Bernstein – the Watergate journalists – on the Internet; investigative journalist, gossip-monger, techno-newshound. Drudge will go down in history as the man who broke the Monica Lewinsky story – if the sordid tale ever reaches the history books. Drudge provides instant inside information on what is happening in the American corridors of power. As we write, Drudge is reporting that the Oscar-winning filmmaker, former Vice President, Al Gore actually wastes more electricity in his home during one month than the average family uses in one year.

Inside information is commercial gold. Companies spend billions of dollars seeking to capture information about their customers. 'Loyal customers are the spoils of the information wars and those who own the customer information own the market,' said Sean Kelly, when he was managing director of the Data Warehouse Network.

But it is not only information about money that is more valuable than money itself. Information about products, services and just about anything that you can think of is worth more than the underlying offering. And it is not only the amount of information that is crucial, but its timeliness and accuracy – one of the reasons why Google has been so successful. Yesterday's news on customer expectations and experiences is simply history. Today's news on customer expectations and experiences is tomorrow's profits.

Competence-based Competition

Brainpower dominates modern corporations. It is their essence. We are increasingly competing on competence. Companies are being transformed, whether they like it or not, from manufacturing companies with a little service to service companies with a little manufacturing. Today, all companies are, or should be, brain based.

Think of how big General Motors is. In terms of revenues, it is still one of the largest companies in the world (with revenues of $192,604 million as compared to Microsoft's paltry $39,788 million). It has thousands of buildings and warehouses; it has huge sophisticated machines. It has been around a long time and in 1996 assembled 647,000 people, the population of a decent-sized city, to do its work. Employee numbers have now shrunk to around 335,000, but that is still a lot of people. Even without vehicle sales it would still rank among the top 30

Fortune 500 companies. Yet, Microsoft outstripped it without apparently breaking sweat. Microsoft doesn't have as many offices, warehouses or machines as General Motors. It doesn't employ as many people. In fact, the only asset of Microsoft is human imagination. It is brain powered.

Yes, the price of oil is up, the price of steel is up, the price of a cup of tea is up, but (in real terms) commodities are now worth one-fifth of their former price.

The good thing about General Motors is that it looks like a big business. With its office blocks, real estate, legions of people and huge factories, it is what we imagine big business to resemble. Our image of corporate perfection is locked in the past – reflected in accounting procedures, management principles, generic strategies, office architecture, use of language and so on. At least the past gave you something to hold onto. The trouble with intellectual capital, brainpower, or whatever you choose to call it, is that it is ethereal and elusive. It becomes a theoretical exercise. You have to *imagine* the firm and its market. We even lack a proper language to describe knowledge. For all the checklists and models, calculating the power of the brains assembled in a room, let alone a corporation, is close to impossible. It is difficult to explain, describe and evaluate. Still, we must persevere in our pursuit of knowledge – after all, love is also difficult yet we continue to try.

'We are always 18 months away from failure,' says Bill Gates. If Microsoft is perpetually teetering on the abyss, what hope can there be for the rest of us?

The new hard currency is information. As Nicholas Negroponte of MIT's Media Lab puts it: 'We are moving from a world of atoms into one of bits.' We are moving from brawn to brain; from hired hands to hired heads. Competition is about kilobytes, not kilograms.

Negroponte is founder and chairman of the One Laptop per Child non-profit association.

Yet, many of us are stuck in the world of atoms. We continue to measure atoms as if they were still the most important things in life. The trade agreement GATT (General Agreement on Tariffs and Trade, now superseded by the World Trade Organisation) is mainly about atoms – about how many tons of a certain good we can move from one geographical location to another. While information travels across borders at the speed of light, few politicians seem to be that bothered. Our balance sheets are about atoms – machines, buildings, etc. – but do we really capture the most critical assets by measuring that stuff?

In our new age, being elusive is good. If you can touch something, it is probably not worth a great deal. What is valuable at Volvo, the car manufacturer that was acquired by Ford Motors in 1999, you cannot touch. The manufacturing facilities are not worth a great deal and the company's headquarters and the warehouse in Holland are nothing more than real estate. What is valuable is the intangible – the Volvo brand, the relationships, the knowledge that exists within the company, the concepts and ideas. Ford had to pay $6.45 billion for all this – a little more than what 4 per cent of America Online ($149.8 billion) would have cost them. Dealers in and of atoms are in for some pretty tough times.

Of course, you can't win them all: AOL merged with Time Warner in 2001. AOL Time Warner reported a loss of $99 billion in 2002 – the largest loss ever reported by a company at the time. Even so, Time Warner's market cap in November 2006 was $80 billion. Ford's market cap is $16 billion.

The value of intangibles affects every business and every aspect of our society and personal lives.

Take a human being, break him down to the smallest of components – atoms. Bring that stuff to the commodities market in Chicago and try to sell it – if you are lucky you will get two bucks. Instead, reassemble the person. Do some surgical engineering and call him Oprah and ask for an annual salary of many, many millions.

Take some water, add sugar, carbonate it, and pour it into a can. The cost is probably less than a quarter. Write Coca-Cola on the can and you can charge a dollar.

Take a cardboard box, a small booklet and a CD-ROM. Together it is probably worth some $5. Write MS Office on it and you can charge $200.

In the brain-based society, perception is all; the intangible is made real by the shrill sound of cash registers. In the brand-based society, Bacardi-Martini paid £1.5 billion ($2.4 billion) for Dewar's four distilleries, 49 employees and a 15-year supplier contract. The company also got the White Label scotch whisky, Bombay Gin and Bombay Sapphire Gin brand names. When the Swedish government decided to sell V&S in 2007, the company was valued at $6–7 billion. For what? A bottle and a name, Absolut. Content of the bottle – hardly any value at all. Strange? Maybe not if you consider the list of some of the most valuable brands in the world:

No wonder that Bernd Pichtesrieder, former CEO at BMW, reflected that he was not really the one who ran the company. He had someone on top of him. The BMW brand on top of the headquarters building, and its heavy weight of history, was the company's real leader. (Now he is CEO of VW and has the same boss.)

Brand	Brand Value ($ million)
Coca-Cola	67,000
Microsoft	56,926
IBM	56,201
GE	48,907
Intel	32,319
Nokia	30,131
Toyota	27,941
Disney	27,848
McDonalds	27,501
Mercedes	21,795

Source: International Best Global brands value 2006

Intelligence and intangibles go hand in hand. But intangibles cost. God does not hand out great brands. Great brands are created – and it takes time. With the exception of Absolut Vodka, how many hot new liquor brands are you aware of? Quite often the information cost – what it takes to attract the interest of oversupplied and increasingly demanding customers – surpasses the

Absolut ignited a trend for imaginative branding in the drinks industry. In recent years we have seen Bacardi Breezers and Vodka Ice come to the fore, plus all the new vodka brands.

actual costs of producing the customer offering. Just think of Coke, Metallica, Gucci, Madonna, Prada or Tiger Woods.

EVERYWHERE: THE LINKED SOCIETY

The reality is that we all live in a borderless world. Most of us are so used to the idea of internationalisation that we take it for granted. Look at the clothes you are wearing. As we write, one of us is wearing pants from Germany, shoes from Italy, a shirt from Canada, and the other is in a pair of pants from the US and a Belgian T-shirt, wearing glasses from Japan. You might think that we cheated – putting on our global costumes in preparation – but we swear to you (on the embalmed body of Lenin) that we are just wearing what everyone else is wearing, albeit only in black. Look around. How many nations do your clothes originate from? We bet that unless you are currently in bed, you would get into serious trouble by taking off all the clothes not made in your home country.

On the other hand, 'Made in the USA' is increasingly meaningless. So, too, is 'Made in Japan' or 'Made in Swaziland'. Nokia has labs in Scandinavia, Japan, Hong-Kong, Germany, Australia, the UK and the US. It sends its people to Venice Beach in LA and King's Road in London to pick up the latest fashion signals. Are its products Finnish? If the nation state is now a meaningless unit of measurement, attribution to a particular nation is also redundant. Interestingly, it is the older generation that remains loyal to nationally produced goods. The British buy British, the French buy French and the Americans buy American out of long-held habit. It is an expression of patriotism. The young couldn't care less. Today, it's made by BMW, made by Nokia, made by Alessi, made by Philippe Starck. What matters is who – not where. It's *made by* or *designed by* – not *made in*.

Globalisation is no longer a theory. It affects nation states, firms, products, services and individuals. And it affects them now, simultaneously. Local used to be the norm and international the exception. Business schools used to have special departments for international business. RoW used to mean the rest of the world. Any company that still uses this acronym should close its doors and admit defeat before they are forcibly closed by dissenting customers. Now, one small department for local business is more appropriate. Why do governments have separate Ministries of Foreign Affairs when most governmental affairs are international? The new institutions cut across geographical boundaries. There are megastates, such as the EU, APEC, NAFTA; multinational firms that are legally local, but operatively global; global products such as Coca-Cola and the Big Mac; global super-specialists; and a host of global musicians, consultants, chefs, researchers, actors, and many more.

True internationalisation – rather than the false alarms we have had in the past – means that a tailor in Wuhan, China is genuinely competing with one in Berlin. There is techno-economic parity – knowledge dissemination means that people in the West no longer have knowledge monopolies so the tailor in Wuhan can quickly have access to the same technology as the tailor in Berlin. The spirit of capitalism is on the move. It has been since it left Europe at the end of the nineteenth century to pay a visit to the USA. Then, it kept going West to end up in the Far East. It is still moving westwards, waving its

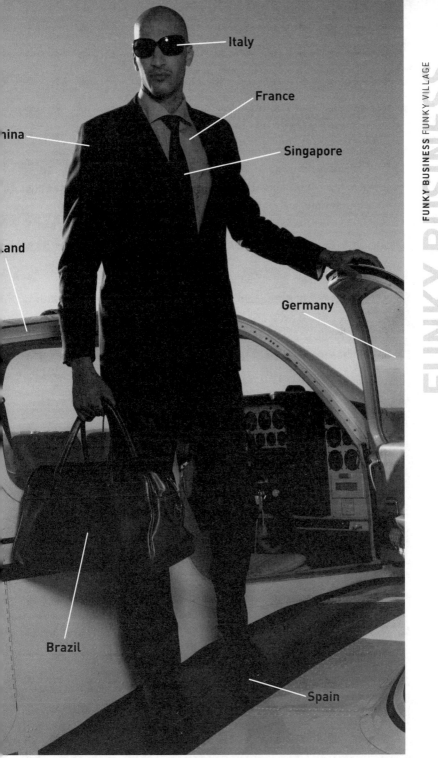

Italy

France

Singapore

China

Land

Germany

Brazil

Spain

magic wand over China and the former USSR. The new reality is developing everywhere. The new economy is multi-centric.

The Far West

Look West. Look to the Far West because that it where the future is unravelling. Many more new jobs are created in the US than in Europe. But the US economy is peculiar in that only certain regions, industries, and companies are extremely dynamic. California, not surprisingly, is one of the clusters of growth. This is a strange place where 40 per cent of the population never use knives and forks for eating, preferring to eat with their hands while standing up. So, international competition seems to be a battle between those who eat with sticks, those who use a knife and a fork, and the supposed sophisticates who merely use their hands. They may use their hands for eating, but their heads drive the economy.

This is a bits, tits and ass economy – Sillywood (Silicon Valley + Hollywood) rules and tittytainment is the name of the game. Much of what is interesting in the US, at least from a business perspective, is linked to the expanding entertainment cluster. While more films are produced by the European Union countries combined than by the United States, the US films have a 71 per cent market share in Western Europe. Don't be fooled, however. Entertainment does not only mean Arnold Schwarzenegger movies or Beyoncé CDs.

Arnold Schwarzenegger became Governor of California in 2003. We certainly would not have wanted to predict that.

Films, music, electronic toys, videos and computer games merge with all aspects of IT – hardware and software, telecommunications, the net and so on – into a highly potent brew.

The US economy leads the way in creating a true information economy. For instance, the US spends 4 per cent of its GDP on IT, while Japan spends only 2 per cent. The US economy is getting softer by the hour. At the height of the dot-com boom, Silicon Valley companies were valued at four times

In 2004, the US invested 4.6 per cent of GDP in Information and Communication Technology – ICT. By contrast, Europe invested 3 per cent. Japan has invested less in ICT than some countries, spending just under 3 per cent of GDP in 2003. This is behind the United States, Australia and Korea, which spent about 4 per cent of GDP, but ahead of France, Germany and Ireland, where ICT investment was below 2 per cent of GDP.

those of Detroit; and their value almost equalled that of the entire French stock market. Palo Alto, California, a place formerly known for its bowel-bindingly delicious prunes and raisins, is now home to thousand upon thousands of electronics and software firms. What's good for General Motors increasingly does not appear to be good for America.

The Far East

Nevertheless, it would be wrong to say that the future is developing only in the Far West. The Far East has exploded in economic growth during the past 10 to 20 years. During the eighteenth century it took Great Britain some 60 years to double its GDP, says Professor Jeffrey D. Sachs of Harvard University. Sachs notes that a hundred years later, Japan managed to do it in half that time. More recently, South Korea did it in 11 years. Back in 1960, the standard of living for the average Japanese citizen was one eighths of that of an American. Economically, South Korea was at the same level as Sudan, and Taiwan equalled Zaire in GDP per capita terms. The World Bank has estimated that as much as 50 per cent of future worldwide growth during the forthcoming decades will be located in South East Asia.

The Far East comes with a positive yearning for education. Some time ago, kids from all around the world were asked whether going to school was one of their favourite activities. In

China 34 per cent said that it was. In Japan 28 per cent agreed. The equivalent number for the US was 18 per cent. Before he passed away, Peter Drucker noted that 'India may already have the greatest engineering and medical schools in the world.'

Even so, the magnitude of the shift remains underestimated. The West is in denial. Some people believe that the economic crisis in the Far East in the 1990s finally proved them right. A Merrill Lynch study shows that in places such as Singapore, Hong Kong and Taiwan, more than 60 per cent of GDP stems from service-related activities. Many of the economies are already knowledge based. We were recently told that a country like Singapore – once described by author William Gibson as 'Disneyland with the death penalty' – spends 25 per cent of its GDP on education, research and development. Those guys have a plan. But of course, Singapore could be wrong. What if we are not going through a revolution? What if knowledge isn't going to be a key asset in the future? Dream on.

In South East Asia, much of the manufacturing is now carried out in China – a country that annually produces more than 600,000 engineers with an average monthly salary of slightly above $500. China has more high-school graduates than America (by a couple of hundred million) and includes 413.7 million people who are under 20. The Chinese are young, educated and greedy. Chinese people are almost like us: while we want to *get* rich they want to *be* rich. A survey showed that some 66 per cent of the Chinese population have this as their prime driving force. A paltry 4 per cent want to continue the great Communist revolution. Until the early nineteenth century

The local company Ningbo Bird already brands and sells more cell phones in China than either Nokia or Motorola. It is also regarded as the fashion leader. In 2007 Ningbo Bird signed a memorandum of understanding with Siemens to cooperate on future mobile phones.

the Chinese economy was the largest economy in the world. If growth continues for the next few years, in 2010 it will have regained its position as the dominant economy on Planet Earth.

Naturally, the impact of Asian competition will change over the coming years. Pure brute-force competition will be complemented by brain-force competition. We can probably learn a great deal from the evolution of Japan as an industrial power. In the beginning, the Japanese made things that were cheaper; the West dismissed them as inexpensive plastic crap. Then, they progressed to make things that were also better. The West made the mistake of assuming the old joke applied. It didn't. As the Japanese killed off most Western electronics companies and slaughtered virtually all the automotive companies, Westerners almost choked on their laughs. Malicious pleasure over the Asian crisis may be similarly shortlived as billions of brains start banging on the door to the West. Just wait, after pleasure comes pressure.

The Close(d) East

Travelling to the Far West or Far East is not enough. The future is also in the Close(d) East. Some of these economies have undergone tremendous changes since the fall of the Berlin Wall in 1989. A few years ago, the Hungarian Economic Minister gave a speech to a group of journalists in which he explained why Communism fell. He provided a long and detailed macroeconomic explanation. When he was done his wife, who happens to be one of Hungary's many new entrepreneurs, rose from her chair and said: 'I'm not sure I understand what my husband just told you, but I will tell you, my friends and I want to go shopping.'

We can look at the Close(d) East using four complementary perspectives. No. 1, for some companies, Eastern Europe is an enormous mess – little infrastructure, organised crime, a different mentality, etc. No. 2, for others Eastern Europe is a gigantic output market – Mercedes sells a lot of luxury cars in Moscow. No. 3, these countries make up a tremendous input market – there is a mega brain-sale in these countries, particularly of people who used to work in the defence industry. No. 4, a few countries have become fantastic tourist havens.

It is notable that some Russian companies no longer hire people from the West because, they say, Westerners are not capitalist enough. They argue that the comfortable citizens of the West are not prepared to work as long hours, as hard, and to bend the rules as much when this is necessary. The Eastern Europeans remain hungry.

Near Here

Unexpected things are happening in Western Europe too. Who would have thought that one of the great companies in the software industry – the funkiest of industries – would be German and called SAP? Where did Nokia – maker of the sexiest and most stylish mobile phones on the market – come from? Today, Finland exports more electronics than forestry products. The Finns also have more Internet hosts per capita than almost any other country. Only Iceland and the US have more. Ten years ago, who would have anticipated that three of the world's hottest airlines would be from the British Isles? Now, just look at easyJet, Virgin and Irish Ryanair.

Europe also offers a number of multicultural role models from soccer teams to entire countries. Some of the most thriving and international of companies are headquartered in multi-ethnic and multi-religious Switzerland. Companies like Nestlé, Ciba Geigy and ABB appear to handle diversity more easily and positively than others in Europe. ABB's supervisory board of eight includes five nationalities. Its former chief executive Percy Barnevik argues that: 'Competence is the key selection criterion, not passport.' Other multinationals are similarly diverse as they discover the twin challenges of globalisation and team working. After its merger, the medical/biotech company SmithKline Beecham boasted a management group of 13 that included seven nationalities. Europe strikes back.

Etc.

We could go on. The economy is growing in a multitude of places. There is no longer a single centre of gravity; there are many. The Western project – a little pink house with a white fence, a

Keep in mind that only 20 per cent of world output is open to global competition. In 30 years, however, it will be 80 per cent.

reliable car, a good-looking wife or husband, nice kids, annual summer vacation to the Mediterranean or the Caribbean, and a decent, steady job – is no longer challenged by only 200 million people. It is no longer just Japan breathing down Western necks. Today, 3,000 million people want to have what most Westerners already have – and they want it now. And, trust us, they won't say please. Frightening? On the contrary. This is the greatest business opportunity of the new millennium. The positive scenario is, of course, that these 3 billion individuals will all soon be potential customers. Supply and demand!

But the funky village is not only global – it is globally linked. Remember the fishnet and the cobweb – changes spread and can be felt everywhere. A market economy is not a zero-sum game. If people in Asia suffer from a recession, that does not improve the standard of living for people in the West in anything but relative terms. If growth in the US economy skyrockets, that's not bad news for anyone on this planet. We are building the international interlinked society together. The funky village means more competition, but it also means more opportunities – opportunities to find new customers, suppliers, partners, experts and friends. The price for not being linked, however, is extremely high.

Leaders and Laggards

Clearly, not all regions are growing at the same rate. According to the World Bank's economic experts, people in fast-growing economies simply work harder, study harder and save more. Economic success and progress are about simple things: working, studying and saving – no magic powder or wand will do the trick.

In the funky village, the game revolves around effectiveness, creation and revolutionary changes; new customer offerings; being completely different; surprising people; providing amazing stuff. Success comes from exploring the unknown and getting it roughly right.

Players with different profiles will dominate throughout the life cycle of any era. In the funky village, there is one region characterised by highly individualistic values. It has institutions that allow for a fluid, temporary and mobile labour market. A region that accepts uncertainty and is a creator of new technology – the United States. So we should not be surprised that American firms now dominate at the beginning of this new era – particularly when collectivism, lifetime employment, uncertainty reduction and the assimilation, rather than creation, of new technology mark one of the main contenders – Japan.

It will not necessarily remain the case. Playing world police comes with a hefty price tag. America's long boom is not written in tablets of stone. Its dominance may not end right away, but it will certainly be challenged. Increased globalisation and value-fusion will have their say. Many people are no longer trapped by geography. Certain Japanese, Danish or Portuguese people are more individualistic creators and uncertainty embracers than the typical American is. The world is now their stage. They are free to exercise their right to choose. And choices they will make. So, we should expect faster and unexpected comebacks as these individuals pick up signals and ideas from one region and transplant them to another. In a placeless society, individuals and organisations with many homes should not be confused with nation states that cannot be cut loose and shipped off somewhere else. Once again, *who* appears more important than *where*.

Europe is a new melting pot. Europeans typically live in countries where 15 to 25 per cent of people have foreign backgrounds. The mix is everything. There are no longer any closed, homogenous, sheltered societies. Living alongside people with different values and value systems is now a fact of life. Of course, all is not sweetness and light. Some societies are more nationalistic than others. No one ever said that living together would be without tension.

Europe needs a dream – a dream that is fundamentally different from the American dream. The problem is that the European Union was founded on the wish to avoid another nightmare: not another big war.

The result is that Europe has a potential diversity advantage – an advantage in that diversity is the mother of creativity, invention and progress. But are the Europeans sitting on top of a powder magazine or a melting pot? Europe has a long history of hostility and rivalry. Its people are used to living in disunity. Is this an asset or a liability? According to the German academic Jurgen Habermas, Europe's heritage definitely works to its advantage when trying to develop the means of handling disunity – a supranational democracy; the European Union. Practice makes perfect.

Still, past developments in the Balkans make even the most optimistic person think twice about the dangers of diversity. But remember, what is, is. Europe is – and has been for centuries – heterogeneous in race, religion, and every conceivable dimension. Diversity per se is not necessarily good or bad – it just is. Diversity becomes what we make of it. Europe does not necessarily need more or less diversity. Europe needs to make up its mind what to do with it. Europe needs a dream, an idea, a new manifesto – words and action. Europeans need to make up their minds as to how to maximise the potential of their heterogeneous population by using advances in technology, institutions and values. Or else, the other players in the funky village will shape Europe's destiny.

THE MIGHTY TERMITES

There are not only changes in time, space and mass. Entering the age of abundance, the world is metamorphosing, taking on new and unclear shapes. Things are drifting, torn apart and recombined in unconventional ways – *panta rei* – to create a blurred, fragmented and hyphenated world.

Our society is left in a state of confusion. Empowered individuals, talent holders, individuals who have the power of choice inhabit this state of confusion. They are people who are free to know, go, do and be whoever they want to be. These individuals, who exercise their right to choose, are creating this age of 'anarchy'. They tear down walls and undermine traditional bases of power. They take control over their education, careers and lives. They initiate system-wide changes that transform the world into a hyper-pluralistic place.

Yesterday, strong centres of power dominated society and our lives. In the 1848 *Manifesto of the Communist Party*, the authors wrote that the aim was to create a society: 'In which industrial production is no longer directed by individual factory owners, competing against one another, but by the whole of society according to a fixed plan and according to the needs of all.' This was the extreme of social engineering with all its assumptions of predictability, stability and control. Driven by an overall vision of the good life, it was just a matter of getting the central plan, structures and systems right. Conservative politicians, capitalists and business managers in the West may have laughed at these utopian aspirations, but were their visions really any better?

We built our own huge, monolithical and centrally planned structures. Some of them we called corporations. A little more than 35 years ago, Harvard economist and advisor to JFK, John Kenneth Galbraith, admitted that: 'We have an economic system which whatever its formal ideological billing is in substantial part a planned economy. Initiative in deciding what is to be produced comes not from the sovereign consumer... Rather it comes from the great producing organization which reaches forward to control the market that it is presumed to serve.' Once again, it was just a matter of getting the structures, systems and strategies – the great master plan – right. In capitalism and Communism alike, there were elements of central planning – in political, social, and economical terms. Some took the decisions and the others obeyed, or were at least told to obey.

If the Old World was a well-structured place filled with castrated individuals, the reality of our times is an unstructured world populated by capable individuals (and some who still seem to prefer eunuch-like uncertainty reduction). Termites have been let loose within our structures and are running amok.

Today, as the poet William Butler Yeats once wrote, the centre cannot hold. Equipped with new technologies and values, entrepreneurial individuals challenge the conventional institutions and purveyors of power. Note that it is not technology, institutions or values that create the New World. The changes, or elements of confusion, that we are experiencing are caused by individuals who no longer accept being told what to know and do, where to go and who to be.

But what may be interpreted as chaos on the societal level is anything but chaotic to these individuals. It is only natural.

THE BLURRED SOCIETY

In the blurred society traditional divides are becoming ever more disordered. Barriers are disappearing and things are floating. We created and used our traditional structures to sort stuff into neat little piles of similar elements. By categorising things we reduced uncertainty. Some were sellers – others buyers. We all agreed on that. Some were banks and others insurance companies. Nothing strange about that. Some were wholesalers and others retailers. Some were liberals and others socialists. Some studied and others worked. Our world was like a deck of cards and we had agreed upon (or been told to use) only one principle for sorting the cards.

Now, the three drivers of change open up possibilities for creative people to restructure, re-sort and reclassify basically every little aspect of our socio-economic landscape. Nothing is given. The entire pack of cards is in the air. Previously, we have talked about blurring geographical and moral boundaries, but the effects can also be seen in a variety of other phenomena. Some companies have even put the blur in their logo.

Industries are blurring. Given that entry barriers are falling as a consequence of internationalisation, deregulation and digitisation, it is easier for firms to make cross-overs. Companies using a new logic enter industry after industry, because to them traditional industrial boundaries make little or no sense. On the surface, they may look like old conglomerates, but in reality they are distinctively different. The underlying idea is that their *capabilities*, not their physical resources, can be used to compete in several industries. Much of the tangible stuff is left to suppliers from all over the world. Just look at the likes of Lego, Virgin or Harley Davidson. In addition, by focusing more on the needs of the demanding customer, rather than the actual product offering and

Where does the firm end and where does it begin?

historical definitions, companies that used to be regarded as players in different industries are beginning to compete. Today, who can tell a bank from an insurance company? They basically provide the same kind of service. From the point of view of the hard-to-please consumer, traditional distinctions are absolutely meaningless. They just want funky business.

Relationships between companies are blurring. If we actually start paying our customers for their attention, just who is the customer? Right now, sellers are also buyers and buyers are sellers. Consider the case of Swedish retailer IKEA. The company sits in the middle of a web of relationships. It has outsourced assembly to customers who want to save a buck or two hundred. True co-production. In effect, the customers are also suppliers. IKEA has left component manufacturing to grateful suppliers who are also customers, gaining access to databases and expert advice. Conclusion: it is getting increasingly difficult to decide whom to invite to the company's Christmas party. Where does the firm end, and where does it begin? The legal boundaries are becoming less relevant and less important. Our relationship to one and the same organisation may well simultaneously contain elements of competition, cooperation, supplying and buying. Co-producing promiscuity is the new reality.

Production and consumption merge into *prosumption*. One of us recently bought a new Volvo car. He initiated the process by producing a list of specifications; what colour, engine, stereo, upholstery, finance deal, etc. he was looking for. Then, Volvo took this list of specs to produce the car that he and his family wanted to consume. Buyers and sellers work together in a circular process. IT opens up opportunities for even more prosumption. Just consider the active part we take when dealing with Amazon.com – providing implicit input about demand and the mix of books, allowing it to track virtual shopping baskets and give tips, or more explicitly in co-creating competitiveness by sending in feedback or book reviews. The company has even regularly paid $1,000 (in book vouchers) to the best amateur critic.

Products and services are also blurring. It is now more accurate to talk about *provices* and *serducts*, as you can hardly separate the two. Atoms and bits coexist in most modern customer offerings. Think of the finance deals accompanying most capital goods we buy (or lease). Think of the pre-packaged 'products' we are offered from financial institutions. Is a Big Mac meal at McDonald's a service or a product? It is both.

The traditional distinction between leisure and work is becoming increasingly blurred. If 70 to 80 per cent of the work that people perform in a modern organisation is done by way of their intellects, is not work a process that goes on continually – 168 hours per week? People do not stop thinking just because they leave the office. Many people even work while sleeping. Ideas are processed in our dreams. This development also makes the classical distinction between home and office less relevant. In the blurred society, work is no longer a place – it is an activity.

Everywhere we look we see blur – East–West, Men–Women, Structure–Process, Right–Wrong. And we experience blur at multiple levels – society, organisations and individuals. But remember, things look blurred only to those stuck in the logic of the past. To those who welcome the funky village there is nothing particularly mysterious about this trend. It is a fact of life. These entrepreneurial individuals and organisations look upon the changes they initiate as restructuring and innovation rather than chaos and confusion.

THE FRAGMENTED SOCIETY

Out of focus it may be, but our world is also being torn apart. It is fragmenting. This, perhaps not surprisingly, is generally regarded as a bad thing. This is not necessarily true – especially not from the point of view of the individual. Fragmentation is largely caused by our wish to belong to and associate with a certain group of people – our desire not to be a commodity, standardised and exactly like the others. If people have indeed been given the power of choice we should not be surprised (or ashamed) that they make different choices.

Society has always been fragmented. But, in the funky village, fundamentally new divides are created. In the not so distant past, we were separated along the lines of blood and proximity. The manuscript for what role we were supposed to play was largely determined by our family and geography. We could act only within neatly defined boundaries and parameters that told us who we were and what to expect of life. Now, new factors come into play. Depending on the level of abstraction, we can spot at least three different types of increased fragmentation.

Polarisation

Polarisation is increasing. Some 300 hundred years ago, wealth was a question of controlling land. Then capital became the thing. No more.

The first of the new apartheids is education. There is a growing gap between the educated and the uneducated. These are the new classes, and this is the new class society. Without unique skills, you are totally exchangeable, and therefore also in direct competition with more than two billion Chinese and Indians. The gap between the employed and the unemployed is increasing. Hardly surprisingly, the rich are getting richer, and the poor poorer. We are on our way toward a 2/3 type of society in which a large portion of people are constantly losing ground.

At a global level there is a growing gap between north and south – 80 per cent of all consumption is made by 20 per cent of the population on Planet Earth. It is a global village with exceptions.

Markets are mechanisms for sorting the efficient from the inefficient; exports are the creative lubricant between the bust and the rust.

We see a similar development between old and young. Most young people certainly don't want to end up like their parents, having a steady job in a big organisation where you get a gold watch and a pat on the back after 40 years of loyal service. That, to a large extent, is human nature. But in terms of skills the differences between young and old people have never been as great.

The second new apartheid is an IT one – and it is binary. One executive told us that there are two kinds of people – A.C. and B.C. – after computers and before computers. Those under 25 have not experienced an IT revolution, but an evolution. They were born with it. To many of them the personal computer is the most natural thing in the world. Either you're in or you're out. These young individuals pose new and different questions of life and work. They want to change the very definition of their jobs. Instead of living to work, they work to live.

Even so, there are still people who say that values never really change, and that things stay the same. This can be easily disproved: just take a look at the cover of a 1960s *Playboy* and compare it to a current front-page of *Elle* or *Cosmopolitan*.

Tribalisation

We all grew up in a world in which geography mattered and proximity ruled. If you were born in Nice, there was an extremely strong likelihood that you would be raised in Nice, go to school in Nice, get a job in Nice, meet your spouse (who also came from Nice) in Nice, buy a house in Nice, have kids in Nice, retire to Nice, die in Nice and finally be buried in Nice. Maybe, if you were really adventurous and could afford it, you would go to the Alps on vacation every now and then. Our old society was geographically structured and so were the tribes. We had the Sydney tribe, the Stuttgart tribe and the Stockholm tribe.

Then forces of funk reshaped our world. The funky village is biographically structured. The new tribes are global. They develop with the people who are relevant to you, no matter where they are. Global *blood-based* tribes have been around for centuries – the Jewish tribe and overseas Chinese. Now, we also see *attitude-based* and *competence-based* tribes. Thanks to globalisation and digitisation, place is no longer

Geography = culture = religion = identity (= indicates sign for 'is not')

relevant. What are Greenpeace, Amnesty International, Hells Angels or hip-hoppers but global biographical tribes made up of people from anywhere in the world? The same goes for MBAs, architects, hackers, engineers and musicians who draw their skills (and attitudes) from global communities. These tribes have their own languages, dress codes, signs, symbols, totems and rituals.

The tribal pioneers are often found in groups considered outcasts and marginal in the geographically structured world. They are people who had great difficulties in finding enough like-minded people in their own neck of the woods. They were basically forced to search globally in pursuit of their tribe. Perhaps we should all learn from the gay community, the Mafia, illicit drug-traders, masochists and the eco-tribe, because in the funky village your tribe is determined by biography not geography, by choice rather than proximity.

Individualisation

If we take this trend one step further, we face total fragmentation and extreme individualisation. The good news is that the opportunities for self-realisation have never been as great. In principle, we can all become as unique as our own fingerprints, as unique as we were really meant to be. The pundits claim that we are entering a ME, ME, ME type of world – the selfish society; an egocentric economy. But individualism

Hip-hop tribal chief P-Diddy

does not necessarily imply egoism. It has more to do with self-realisation – being a whole person. For better or for worse, each individual becomes a micro cosmos of supply and demand in a global market.

Loyalty, in this environment, is re-cast. The global knowledge worker, part of the new elite, is loyal to him- or herself and the tribe, rather than the (temporary) employer. In a casino loyal economy these people will link up and cooperate only with those who will prove beneficial to them. They will form global tribes that will roam the world as 'overnight armies of intellectual mercenaries', as MIT's Thomas Malone puts it. They will buy only from those organisations that are compatible with the values of their own tribe – those who share the same vibe.

From a business point of view it is crucial to understand that the group of 'lead customers', those who represent the needs and requirements of consumers in the future, will not only consist of knowledge workers and the rich. Men and women with a degree in science, an MBA and a promising career may consume more than the rest of the population. But more consumption does not necessarily imply more foresight or insight. Quality does not follow from quantity.

We were all brought up with the notion that patient, cautious acquisition was the way to gradually build a better life. Today, consumers will often be drawn from the downwardly noble – people who may not have all the money in the world, but spend every single cent on one thing. They focus on acquiring the symbols that are critical to their tribe or themselves. They sacrifice everything to get the latest and funkiest mountain bike, travelling experience, surf board, bottle of wine (perhaps not the latest one in this case), DVD player, yoga class, or whatever. This is where we should look if we want a glimpse of the future, not to those who excel in average spending capability.

Not everyone will join the individualistic acquisition frenzy. Some will get lost in the funky village. Not because they do not fit in, but because they will exercise their right to say no. And some will choose to deny what is happening. These groups will undoubtedly fight back through extreme localisation and increased hostility against IT, dissidents and the overall fusion in values. Reactionaries can be found in any camp – business people and executives who still believe in management by fear; fundamental Islamists; neo-nazis and fascists who believe races should be kept apart; men who claim that women are not interested in making careers; politicians who think and act as if markets have not been deregulated.

Change is not friction-free – many of those in command of the present system will fight back. The old does not give in to the new without resistance. Capitalism and democracy now threaten the Communist economy of China. So what do the leaders in Beijing do? Do they shift institutions *en masse*? No. They start making adjustments to the existing institutions by introducing elements of the market economy. Similarly, values have changed so that the likes of divorce, one-parent families and homosexual relationships are accepted. These are value-based innovations that created benefits for many who felt uneasy with the previous

The dramatic decline of social capital appears on the surface to be a bad thing. Places where innovation flourishes, such as Seattle and the Bay area in California, generally have below-average levels of social capital.

norms. Then, disciples of orthodoxy strike back. Just look at the ultra-conservative moral right in the US.

The underlying principles of these wide-ranging examples are the same. Change is not automatic – it is created by individual entrepreneurs.

THE HY-PHE-NA-TED SOCIETY

The future also brings more fusion. Welcome to *hyphe-nation* – a cut and paste culture. If there is a surplus of basically everything that we can imagine, the natural way for people and organisations to escape this excess is to combine things in novel ways. And the weirder the combination, the more unique the result. The realities of our times call for mixing the existing into something exciting – just look at edu-tainment, café-latte, corporate-university, info-tainment, distance-learning, visual-ergonomic, TV-dinners, info-com, psycho-linguistics, bio-tech, e-mail, antibacterial-clothes, gin-tonic and so on.

And hyphenation is omnipresent. You see it in business. Products are increasingly turned into multi-multi-technology offerings. They do everything. A firm such as Canon combines

Now with laser beam

chemistry, electronics and software. For a car company like BMW, innovation is a question of blending mechanics with electronics design and finance skills. L'Oréal mixes pharmaceuticals and fashion when developing its fragrances and lotions. Companies try to capture the attention of demanding customers by offering something more, something new, something surprising.

You see it in music. A hit record in the 1950s was just a song. No more. You see it in the make-up of organisations. In Silicon Valley companies, for instance, traditional 'minority groups' such as women, immigrants and youngsters are dramatically over-represented compared to their status in traditional US firms. You see it in art. The late Luxembourg painter Michel Majerus combined Watteau with Warhol and Walt Disney cartoons. American artist Clay Ketter mixes painting with construction materials and IKEA kitchen cabinets. We see it in architecture, food, sports, education and healthcare. We see it everywhere.

Some will say that hyphenation is the ultimate proof of our lack of imagination. Others suggest that since everything that ever will be invented has been invented, the only way forward is to combine what is already there. The result of both views is that we end up living in an ultra-boring post-modern society.

The other interpretation of hyphenation is that variation in itself breeds even more variation. If certain individuals or companies combine a and b into c, c can then be used to find new combinations with d, e, f and so on. Once it gets going, variation by its very nature increases exponentially.

It is also vital to keep in mind that hyphenation at its best does not mean addition but multiplication – the value created must be more than the sum of the parts combined. In other words, profitable hyphenation requires combining things in such a way that extra value is created. At the same time it needs to be difficult for the customer to unbundle the offering. Because if the customer can easily separate the things that have been combined, he or she can use increasingly perfected markets to get one or all of these items from someone else.

Either we multiply to create the unbundeable or the consumer will go ahead and do the hyphenation.

Let us use a simple example to explain what we mean. One of Kellogg's products is called Choco-Cornflakes. What you get is ordinary cornflakes with chocolate flavour. If the company had just used simple addition, it would have put one bag of cornflakes and one bag of chocolate powder in the cereal box. By pouring the ingredients into a bowl of milk we would get Choco-Cornflakes. Having done this once, it would be easy for us to unbundle the offering and get one box of ordinary cereal and milk chocolate from another supplier. So, Kellogg's uses multiplication. By covering every single cornflake with chocolate, the firm makes it much harder for the consumer to unbundle the product (if you have a lot of time and patience just try it and go bananas). A weird example maybe, but the underlying logic applies to any business or activity. Successful hyphenation requires multiplication – unbundeability.

THE WINNER TAKES ALL

Do you by chance remember Wally Masur? Didn't think so. In the early 1990s, Wally was one of the best tennis players in the world. He was in the top 50 and his career peaked in 1993 when he reached the semi-finals at the US Open, one of the four Grand Slam tournaments. Still, Mr Masur never got a contract to endorse either a tennis shoe or a racket. In comparison with André Agassi or Pete Sampras, Wally Masur was not interesting or good enough for the Nikes and Adidas of the world to contact him. If you can get the best of the best, why settle for anything less? Almost just isn't good enough. Sorry, Wally.

Entering a global excess economy marked by close to friction-free markets, there is a clear risk (or chance) that the winner will take all. In a borderless world, individuals or companies that are perceived as being only 1 per cent better, or those that get a head-start and can use this initial

Winner takes it all

advantage to gain even more reputation and market share, may kill all the others. Just look at Microsoft. Its operating system was perhaps not the best, but the firm managed to establish a world standard, got other software companies to write applications for their system and built in switching costs for all users. (Just imagine the extra costs of changing to a non-Windows-compatible operating system.) Microsoft smartly surfed the waves and, in effect, ended up with (close to) a global monopoly. And the company keeps on surfing the waves – adding on Microsoft Explorer free of charge to crush Netscape – at least until the US government sends out its Baywatch lawyers to close down the beach.

Both things did indeed happen.

We see such developments all over the world. Why listen to the local bard or band when you can get a Madonna, Robbie Williams or Pavarotti CD? Why use a local body-builder in an action movie when people are only interested in Russell Crowe and other global beefcake actors? Why watch a local soccer game when you can watch the best football teams in Europe like Manchester United playing Milan on TV? Why use a second-rate architect for designing your house when you can get the best? Global stars capture all the attention and make ridiculous sums of money.

Ironically, the turbo market capitalism of our times comes with a built-in bomb. In many cases, it will self-destruct. Maybe it won't happen within the next five seconds – reality isn't an episode of *Mission Impossible* – but strong forces eventually push international surplus competition towards global monopolies. We will not see the extreme consequences of this trend in all industries – one bar, one barber, etc. – but particularly when brains, the Net and increasing returns come into play, potential worldwide monopolies await.

There are extreme economies of scale in most knowledge-intensive activities, at least if knowledge can be codified and frozen in atoms. Consequently, the incentives for capturing 100 per cent of a global market are great, and the costs for doing so diminish dramatically the more customers the company can attract. The process accelerates still further if consumer value increases with the number of people who have access to or use what is offered. The Net is perfect for this kind of business, since customers basically participate in the creation of value – prosumption. The more people who visit Yahoo, Amazon et al., the better the service these companies can provide and the more people will come. This explains why so many Internet companies sacrifice short-term profits for growth. Mary Meeker, Internet analyst at Morgan Stanley, said: 'On the web, being No. 1 is awesome, No. 2 is okay, No. 3 is tough, No. 4 is the pits, No. 5 "Huh? Who?"'

Recipe-based Competition

We are entering a world marked by techno-economic parity – dog eat dog days are here. In this surplus society, very few commodities, technologies, products, services, insights, knowledge areas or procedures that can be found in Berlin,

Birmingham, Tokyo, Helsinki and Dallas are not also available to their colleagues in Singapore, Prague, Moscow, Mexico City and Manila. If this is really so, no person or firm can any longer base their sustainable competitive advantages solely on access to abundant resources.

Instead, as Stanford's Paul Romer puts it, the one with the best recipe will win. The individual, tribe, organisation or region that excels in developing innovative concepts and ideas about how to combine and re-combine the ingredients will be most successful. We all need a recipe that is unique enough to capture the attention of oversupplied and demanding customers; a recipe that adds real value; a recipe that is difficult for the others to copy. And, in a winner takes all type of society, we must all realise that if we fail in developing the tastiest of recipes, this may very well be our Last Supper.

What's the best recipe?

'Destroy to build' Mao Zedong

Love them or hate them, companies remain the powerhouses of the capitalist system. 'Corporations are the dominant social institutions of our age,' says Richard Pascale, author of *Managing on the Edge*. Just think of a single fact: the 300 largest multinational companies control 25 per cent of all the productive assets on earth.

Half of world trade is handled by multinational companies. In 2002, the UN Conference on Trade and Development published an article showing that 29 of the world's top 100 economies were multinational businesses rather than countries. Forget the Romans or the British Empire. These global firms are the new empires roaming and running the world.

In this chapter, our beliefs have hardened. Great organisations are based on fantasy, feelings and faith – intellectual capital + psychological capital + social capital, without which organisations are vacuums. So the next time, do your benchmarking against Oxford, Manchester U or the Vatican.

What is impressive about these empires is that they are built around an empty legal entity. Corporations are legal frameworks. They are shells. A company or a business firm basically consists of four different things: *capital*, dollars, nickels and dimes; *machinery* and *buildings*, the dirty and expensive hardware; *people*, the problematic software; and a basic *idea*, the most elusive element of all.

While we salute the massive power wielded by corporations we know that they will look and behave differently tomorrow. In a global, real-time, brain-based and messy world, the inflexible structures of the past do not stand a chance. But funky organisations do not merely adapt to these trends. They are not mirrors, reflecting changes in the environment. Funky organisations build mirrors – mirrors reflecting images that people have never seen before. They enable us to see what was once invisible – what was not. They reshape our perception of what is. Or, to paraphrase George Bernard Shaw's 1903 play, *Man and Superman*: The reasonable organisation adapts itself to the world; the unreasonable one persists in trying to adapt the world to itself. As a result, progress depends on the unreasonable organisation. Ken Olsen, founder of Digital Equipment Corp., phrased it differently – but the sentiments are the same. 'The best assumption to have is that any commonly held belief is wrong.' Success comes from shaping the future. Success is about creation, not adaptation.

Andy Warhol did it. Charlie Parker did it. Michael Dell did it. Muhammed Ali did it. Steve Jobs did it over and over again. They created something new, vibrant and original. They created what was not. Some people were predictably outraged and dismissed them as cranks. But, as Yossarian in Joseph Heller's novel *Catch-22* concludes, 'Of course it's insane... That's why it's the only sane thing to do.' Sanity and sameness are overrated. Art will never be the same. Jazz will never be the same. The computer business will never be the same. Boxing will never be the same. Insight is like a positive HIV. There are no remedies. Once you have it you cannot get rid of it. True entrepreneurs and entrepreneurial organisations offer us the opportunity to take a bite of an apple from the tree of knowledge. Then, there is no way back. Why else did God expel Adam and Eve from paradise?

Something new, vibrant and original

Organisations come and go. They rise and fall. They change shape constantly. They leave the nations and regions in which they were born. They reorganise, realign, refocus. Nothing stays the same. But fear not, Funky Inc. is already here. Funky Inc. isn't like any other company. It is not a dull, old conglomerate. It is not a rigid bureaucracy. It is an organisation that actually thrives on the changing circumstances and unpredictability of our times. Its difference – and its perpetual search for difference – is visible both in terms of its looks and how it operates. Funky Inc. is:

FUNKY INC. IS FOCUSED

Entering the age of abundance, we have to stop believing that organisations can master all things and situations. As long ago as 1776, the economist Adam Smith pointed out that as the size of a market increases, so should the degree of specialisation. Two hundred years later there are no more geographical limits to push. We are there.

Stakeholders, inside and outside the firm, now have the power of choice. They all have access to international markets.

None of them will accept middle of the road models. The excess economy is ruthless. For the demanding customer, only the best will do, and no one can excel at everything. Global competition in an oversupplied world with increasingly perfected markets kills average product offerings and performers.

There are also internal factors that prevent us from spreading our resources too thinly. No matter how much digitisation, globalisation and deregulation we may experience, we are still human beings with limited cognitive capacity. There are studies which show the limits of human receptivity – using all five senses – to be about 10 Mbs. Our brains just don't have the bandwidth to handle excessive breadth. The same studies indicate that the conscious process of information is a maximum of 32 bits per second. There is no way we can attend to everything with the same energy and emphasis.

Then there is the question of the internal climate of the organisation. In non-focused firms and nations, money is often reallocated from winners to losers, leaving people in the profitable businesses disappointed and demotivated. Likewise, there is a risk that the underperformers will doze off and rely on the others to save their necks yet again. Time is spent on political rather than productive matters. A sense of clarity and urgency is lacking.

In a society where money flows freely across borders, the shareholder will accept nothing else than continuous and fantastic value-creation. Increasingly perfected markets and total transparency prevent the pursuit of 'un-natural' synergies. The management team of any diversified organisation is basically saying that it is better than the market at balancing risk and creating value. But actors on the market can now evaluate each business separately. If they come to the conclusion that the sum of the parts is actually greater than the present whole, they will step in and dismantle the company. Why should some overpaid president manage my investments? If I want a diversified portfolio, I will put it together on my own or turn to an expert on such matters. In the meantime we have a very limited understanding of our own limitations — 80 per cent of the population think that they are better than average drivers.

As an effect of increasing customer, employer and shareholder pressure, more and more hierarchies are being engulfed by markets. Perfected markets hate inefficiencies so inefficiencies disappear. Inept organisations are dismembered or they die. So, funky organisations do not aspire to be everything for everyone. Instead, they try to become something for someone. This focus has three elements.

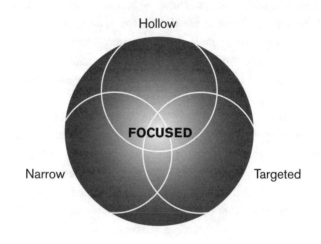

Narrow Focus

Funky Inc. is narrow, focused on one or just a handful of core businesses. One of the reasons why conglomerates became so popular, among theorists as well as practising managers, was the idea of synergy. This was – and depressingly, still is – the ugly stepchild of corporate strategy. The management guru Igor Ansoff first proposed synergy in the 1960s. It is a saddening thought that while the rest of the world enjoyed the overflowing excess of the Summer of Love, managers got down to synergy. Igor Ansoff was no Jimi Hendrix or Jim Morrison, but his message lives on. Managers fell in love with the potent simplicity of his concept. In their minds 2 + 2 really could equal 5. Managers had no need for hallucinogenics.

In retrospect, synergy cast a haze over rational managerial thought. This lingered for quite a while. Synergy gave managers an excuse to manage bigger and bigger companies rather than better and better companies.

Next time you hear the word synergy, cock your guns. Often 2 + 2 = 3.5 instead of 5. Synergy is an expression of the managerial belief that it is much more fun to manage a large company than a small one. After all, you get to make speeches, meet kings and queens, smoke cigars and drink cognac, while presidents of small, excellent companies are left out in the cold – no matter how profitable they are. At a time of local and limited competition, this logic might just have worked – many Third World conglomerates are still successful in their protected home markets. In the kingdom of the blind, the one-eyed man could still be CEO. Today, it will not work. In the face of oversupplied international markets with total competition, we all have to realise that only the best is good enough. If you have stopped believing in Santa Claus, you may as well give up believing in synergies too.

Jim Collins' book *Good to Great* has outsold all earlier management books on this simple recognition – the Level Five leader is humble (and puts the organisation before himself) yet he assembles a team that will not shy away from the most difficult decisions when the truth needs to be heard.

The other classical argument for diversification was that of spreading risk – not placing all your eggs in one basket. But in a world characterised by genuine uncertainty and total unpredictability, we can no longer believe in minimising risk. Indeed, we now need to embrace risk rather than eliminating it. Contemplating the fact that TetraPak, the Swedish packaging giant, had bet its future on one product, former owner Hans Rausing once claimed: 'We minimise risk by maximising risk.'

Put all this together and the message must be that the days of the large and diversified firm are over. In an age of abundance, sharp is beautiful; being sharp and narrow is ravishingly beautiful. The antidote to mindless pursuit of synergies is to become intensely focused on those businesses where you clearly have a global competitive edge. Companies have to be turned from blunt instruments into sharpened precision tools.

Organisations are already honing themselves. How narrow a company is can be measured in terms of Standard Industry Codes (SICs), the number of different industries in which the firm is active. In the late 1970s, the average American firm scored a little more than four SICs, a few years back this measure was down to a little more than two. Translation: the typical US company has lost some 50 per cent of its body parts in less than 20 years. The excess economy is a pretty demanding weight watcher prescribing tough diet programmes. The perfected market functions as a modern-age Dr Frankenstein, cutting off and collecting spare body parts wherever and whosoever they may be.

Hollow Focus

The second characteristic of focused Funky Inc. is that it is hollow. Focusing on only a few businesses just isn't enough. As strategy guru Gary Hamel sometimes puts it, you can take a fat man and cut off one of his legs, but that won't really make him any thinner. Every little process and activity in the firm must be exposed to the question: are we really world class? If not, outsource it. Buy it from someone else – someone who is better. Funky Inc. competes on the basis of its core competence and *competents*, the people who make competencies happen.

In an economy where you can buy most of what the typical company is doing just by Googling, the 'un-hollow' are doomed. In most large cities the Yellow Pages now covers 1,600 rather than 160 pages and new websites with product offerings are added by the second. Surplus again. As noted earlier, globalisation and digitisation combined have dramatically changed the outcome of the classical fight between markets and hierarchies – make or buy. Over time, the odds change. Today, markets rule more than ever. What was logical and sound a few years back is now ludicrous and stupid. What makes sense today will probably not do so tomorrow. It's a never-ending story. Change, then change again.

Imagine that your company is built of Lego. Pick up a piece and ask yourself – are we the best company in the world at information systems – no, that is Accenture or Cap Gemini – so let them take care of it. Are we the best company in the world at cleaning offices – no, that is ISS – so let them take care of it. Are we the best company in the world at accounting – no, that is Ernst & Young – so let them take care of that stuff. It is a simple principle. The logic is even simpler. Sooner or later, and in most cases sooner rather than later, all processes will be exposed to global competition.

Identifying core competencies is navel gazing. Look inside and discover yourself. Soul searching. What are you really good at? What are you better than everyone else at doing? In what ways do these competencies add value, and to which customers? How many of your employees share these competencies? How difficult would it be for your competitors to copy them? These are simple questions but the answers can reshape entire businesses.

Once organisations really start trying to identify their core competencies, many of them realise that these are not always in the areas they thought they would be in. American Airlines, for example, realised that its real strengths were tied to Sabre, the booking system, rather than operating airplanes. In 1995, Sabre alone accounted for 44 per cent of the company's pre-tax profits. GE, IBM, Ericsson and Xerox are all experts in the area of consulting. Their products have become nothing more than bi-products, a sideshow to the main action. Again, we can see the shift from atoms to bits. Atoms just aren't scarce enough so it is increasingly difficult to base competitiveness on access to them.

American spun off Sabre on 15 March 2000 to become a publicly listed company. It is now a privately held company.

Focusing on your core competencies means sticking to what you excel at. Back in 1994, if you drove a Toyota it was only 25 per cent Toyota, whereas a GM car was 47 per cent GM. GM decided to add customer value and create a competitive edge by manufacturing its own car stereos. At Toyota, management argued that other companies such as Sony, Bose or Philips are much better at this so why bother – and then just how important is the car stereo when you buy a new car? We won't embarrass GM with a table depicting its well-managed, gradual decline over the past 20 years.

First quarter 2007, Toyota became the largest automotive company in the world.

Do it well. Do it fantastically well. And then stop. Nike has struck gold by *not* applying its slogan. Instead of just doing it – the company just doesn't do it. Funky Inc. brings in other people to do the rest. Many successful firms no longer make what they sell. Timberland, for instance, is a shoeless shoe-company. Funky Inc. looks like the façades from an old Hollywood motion picture, nice on the outside, virtually empty on the inside save for one thing: brains.

There are exceptions to every rule. Highly successful Spanish fashion company Zara manufactures its own clothes.

Look at the computer company Dell. It is a huge company that has come from absolutely nowhere. It is a huge company in terms of sales, but it does not have a single factory. There is no such place as a Dell factory. What founder Michael Dell realised was that 'IBM took $700 worth of parts, sold them to a dealer for $2,000 who sold them for $3,000. It was still $700 worth of parts.'

By short-circuiting the market, by eliminating unnecessary actors who did not add any value to the customer, he created a business empire. Dell became an intelligent and flexible broker of parts, the professional procurement department of every single customer. 'If this works for computers, it's going to work for automobiles, furniture, carpets, appliances, anything,' said now retired Larry Bossidy – he went on to invite Michael Dell to give a presentation to the management team of his organisation.

You can call this new firm virtual, hollow, a spider's web, outsourced, networked, a shamrock, or whatever you like. The important thing is that if we don't slim down, our chances of surviving and thriving in an excess economy are just that – slim. Call it hollow, but don't call it empty.

An organisation may hollow itself in a number of different ways. Quite often people only think about leaving more stuff to the suppliers – backward disintegration. But hollowing out can also mean handing over activities to the customers – just think of IKEA. The typical Internet banks, for instance, enable us to pay our own bills – forward disintegration. Viewing the company as a collection of Lego pieces, it is basically up to each and every part of the organisation to design its own role in contributing to the value of the whole. It used to be a question of adding stuff – integration. Now we focus on subtracting activities – disintegration and co-creation.

Funky Inc. may not incorporate an entire value chain, but it always has a position. In fact all companies have positions. It is just a question of what we buy and what we make. And by focusing on a few key value-adding processes and eliminating unnecessary actors, we make the rest of the value chain, as well as end-users, extremely dependent on us. And dependence equals dollars.

However, there is something beyond core competencies. What is critical in the funky firm is perhaps not so much the core competencies as the 'core competents'. These are the limited numbers of people at a company who actually embody the skills that make the products and services unique – Mr and Mrs Indispensable. These are the Mick Jagger and Keith Richards of the corporate world. And most of them are way too competent to be wasted in management positions. They are critical because a) they are super-smart, and/or b) they know who is smart, where these people are located and how to get them to cooperate.

Today research indicates that your psychological capital (confidence, hope, optimism and resilience) is more important than your intellectual capital (education and experience).

These 'walking monopolies' will only stay as long as the organisation can offer them something they want. If that is no longer the case they will leave to set up their own one-person companies. Remember that Karl Marx was right. The workers currently own the most critical resources, the major assets of society. While competents personify prospective cores, it is our experience that competencies, at least as popularly defined and used, often represent retrospective scores. Instead of looking into the future, many companies look into the past.

Nathan Myhrworld, formerly with Microsoft and now founder and CEO of Intellectual Ventures, argues that we've got to understand that in a knowledge-based society, the difference between the average and the really good is no longer a factor of 1:2, as it used to be. No, it is a factor of 1:100, or even 1:1,000. His former boss, Bill, sometimes says that if 20 people were to leave Microsoft, the company would risk bankruptcy. Hiroshi Yamauchi at Nintendo, the computer game company, echoed the same line of reasoning. He claimed that an

Want to become a core competent? Learn to use your strengths. Don't spend too much time dealing with your weaknesses.

ordinary person cannot develop a really good game no matter how much he or she tries. Or listen to what Sun Microsystems chairman Scott McNealy has to say about fellow founder Bill Joy: 'AT&T has Bell Labs, and we have Bill Joy. We get a lot more for our money.'

Core competents are omnipresent. In a study by the Corporate Leadership Council, a 'computer' firm recognised 100 core competents out of 16,000 employees; a 'software' company had 10 out of 11,000; and a 'transportation' group deemed 20 of its 33,000 employees as really critical. In other words, the percentage of core competents varied between 0.6 per cent and 0.06 per cent. No wonder that, despite high unemployment rates, so many organisations speak of an ongoing talent war.

Targeted Focus

The third and final element to Funky Inc.'s focus is that it is targeted. Funky where it's based or how large it is. What does matter is that they share a common vibe – values and attitudes.

Violent drug barons create tribes. Miguel Caballero is the Armani of the armoured apparel world. His company sells customised and fashionable bullet-proof clothes. It has targeted a specific tribe. Its home base is Colombia where demand is great.

Pilgrims create tribes. Every year, 75,000 Chevrolet Suburban vans are sold in Saudi Arabia. But why is this country such a huge market for the Suburban? The reason is that the pilgrims who visit Mecca are only allowed to enter the city in a vehicle with specific measurements. The only car that fits the specs happens to be the Chevrolet Suburban. In an unlikely 'holy' alliance a US firm profits from aiding the Muslim tribe.

Leg fetishists create tribes. A while back, we came across a magazine called *Legshow*. It is a global magazine for people obsessed with naked legs and feet. A small market, one would have thought. Surely, foot fetishists cannot form a huge percentage of society. The reality is that the publishers of *Legshow* do very well thank you. Why? It dominates a certain tribe. *Legshow* has developed a profitable

We also draw your attention to another classic case study (as yet not covered by Harvard Business School): *Marquis*, a magazine for latex fetishists.

niche. It does not have a foothold in the market, but has a very large boot covering all of the market – globally. While most magazines die in their infancies, *Legshow* thrives.

The message is that if you focus your energy on creating and then exploiting an extremely narrow niche you can make a lot of money. The tribe may consist of one-legged, homosexual dentists. It may be lawyers who race pigeons. But if you manage to capture these customers globally, you can make a lot of money. In an excess economy, we find riches in niches.

It is easier said than done. You have to get it right. You have to provide exactly the right offering for a clearly identified tribe and then deliver it repeatedly. There may only be 60 *Legshow* customers in Sweden, 55 in Norway, and 96,453 in France, but as we begin to conquer country after country it adds up to a lucrative business. Chris Anderson wrote *The Long Tail* in 2005 to describe how small segments add up to multi-million-dollar businesses.

Forget about legs for a while. A friend of ours recently bought a new car and called all the major insurance companies in Scandinavia to check out what they could offer. Honest to a fault, he confessed to having a lengthy criminal record, drinking a bottle of vodka every day, and never going to bed without smoking pot. To his astonishment, he still hasn't been contacted by any of the companies. This is when we realised that we had stumbled upon the perfect business idea: an insurance company for alcoholics, junkies and criminals.

Of course, the trouble with such brilliantly simple entrepreneurial ideas is that there is often someone else who got there before you. But, surely not. Insurance for junkies and alcoholics? For the dull, unimaginative insurance industry we thought that these would be tribes too far. It is one thing to target 65 year-old retired middle managers with a pension and carefully amassed savings, another to insure the detritus of society. We were wrong.

Progressive Corp. does just that and it is such a good idea that it is now the third largest car insurance company in North America, and one of the most profitable. Naturally, its strategic focus on this tribe is not the only critical success factor. The company has found the key to unlock this goofy niche by being extremely customised. Progressive is always open. Twenty-four-hour service is not just a slogan. When one of its customers crashes – and, given its clientele, this happens from time to time – Progressive rushes to the scene and tries to work things out with the other party. By doing so, it often manages to avoid bringing lawyers into the process. In the litigious US, this means cutting total process costs from an average of $9,400 to $2,100. As a consequence, Progressive can offer decent rates to junkie, former getaway drivers with drinking problems.

Such tidy and lucrative solutions exist in all industries. They may not always be made up of alcoholics, junkies or criminals, but they do exist. We only have to develop a recipe that is tasty enough.

As you'd expect, the founder of Progressive, Peter Lewis, is far from conventional. His 'friends' sometimes call him 'a functioning pothead', 'a frame or two off the ordinary radar-screen', and 'a rock-star without any musical ability'. Peter Lewis is more than 70 years old. He is a core competent. The company is so heavily dependent on him that a few years ago Wall Street analysts wanted to force him to get a physical examination. Peter Lewis didn't really fancy going to the doctors so he sent them a note instead. The note said:

1 'I feel fine.

2 I swim a mile every day.

3 I'm single, so I get laid a lot.'

Of course, nothing is guaranteed. As we were starting to put together *Funky Business Forever* in November 2006, we heard that Peter Lewis had suffered a heart attack at his apartment in New York.

The first wave of funk killed those organisations that were not narrow enough. Conglomerates, where management could not convince the market that synergies were more real than UFOs, were chopped into pieces. The second wave of funk is now ripping process after process and activity after activity out of the bodies of un-hollow corporations. These organisations are forced to adapt or die. And in the not too distant future those companies not targeted on a specific tribe may well be the next victims of funk. Only the focused will flourish.

FUNKY INC. IS LEVERAGED

The second crucial aspect of Funky Inc. is that it is leveraged. In recent years management and corporations have sought to solve the corporate puzzle through an obsession with minimisation. Huge sprawling companies have sought to minimise bureaucracy, numbers of employees, and time. Now, we need to maximise. Simply put, you cannot shrink to greatness. Downsizing easily becomes dumbsizing instead of rightsizing. Companies should not be neutron bombed. Or as Stanford's Jeffrey Pfeffer puts it, 'Downsizing will only do one thing: make the organisation smaller.' There is no way of creating new wealth by simply reducing costs and getting rid of people. Texas chainsaw-massacre management does not result in revenue growth. It has to be lean!

Once an organisation has identified its basic businesses, the core capabilities and the target tribe, it needs to leverage its key resources. Funky Inc. needs to move on from corporate liposuction and anorexia to corporate bodybuilding – getting rid of the fat *and* letting the muscles grow.

In the machine age, leverage often meant real diversification – we needed different machines to make different products. But in a brain-based world, one and the same competence can be used to enter an array of industries, without being involved in the actual production of stuff as such. As noted earlier, the result is blur. The globally linked society forces firms to leverage competence in new ways and increased digitisation enables and opens up the means by which this can happen. As with hollowing, leveraging is a three-stage process.

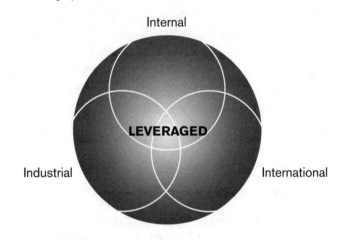

Internal

LEVERAGED

Industrial   International

Internal Leverage

The problem with most organisations is not that they know too little, but that they do not know what they know. Knowledge is dispersed without anyone having a clear picture of the total stock, how and where it flows, or the location of specific capabilities.

To thrive, we must create a learning organisation. This requires us to realise and acknowledge that we are not perfect. Unfortunately, this is often something which managers and companies are unwilling to contemplate. They should perhaps remember Arthur Koestler's definition of creativity as 'a type of learning where the teacher and the pupil are located in the same individual'.

Today the phrase 'learning organisation' has been so misused that learning guru Chris Argyris suggests we test it with its opposite – "the non-learning organisation" – to see if it is relevant. Fashionable phrases should not cloud the fact that we must create a climate that will enhance and speed up learning.

Building a learning organisation is about increasing the rate of knowledge *transfer* and *transformation*. Georgi Lozanov recognised the need already in the 70s with his accelerated learning methods. This starts with leveraging knowledge throughout the firm. We must move knowledge from individual levels to group and organisational levels. This sounds simple, but let us ask you three simple questions:

1 Are some of your colleagues better performers than others?

2 Would you like the others to become as good?

3 What is being done about it?

Learning does not happen automatically; it must be managed. And the speed of a company will be determined not by the fastest and smartest people but by the slowest and least skilled. Enabling learning is one of the key tasks for any leader. Leaders must ensure the continuous transfer of knowledge across organisational boundaries. The individual parts must be able to reflect the whole. In effect, Funky Inc. must work in a similar way to the human brain.

Creating a learning organisation is only part of the story. Customers do not pay companies – not even universities – for their learning abilities. They open their wallets for companies that can teach them something. So, in a real-time world we must decrease the time from insight to output. 'An organisation's ability to learn, and translate that learning into action rapidly is the ultimate competitive business advantage,' says Jack Welch.

Unless the capabilities can be put to good use, they are virtually worthless. But creating such an organisation is costly – IT investments, more travelling, co-location of key people and other measures do not come cheaply. The more important question, however, is whether you can afford not to invest in building a learning organisation. Or as a Scandinavian entrepreneur once put it, 'If you think competence costs – try incompetence.'

Your challenge = turn the corporation's structural capital into your own human capital. Become a vacuum cleaner of competence! Unlike dust, it won't diminish as you suck it up. Suck and see.

As a result, a critical task for any organisation is to turn the core competents into core competencies. The funky firm transforms human capital into structural capital. They collect the knowledge of the gold-collar workers and excellent teams. By building systems containing this competence, the firm provides the others in the organisation with an opportunity to learn and then use their new insights to help customers. Inevitably, this process calls for open communication and discussions throughout the entire company (and the external network). It may well be that the prime denominator of future competitive advantages will be related to which people are allowed to have what discussions about which topics with whom, when, and where. The manager becomes a kind of talk-show host. The question of whether one should try to be the Jerry Springer or the Oprah Winfrey of the firm, we leave to you. Funky Inc. is built around forums, virtual and real, where people can meet, rather than boxes and arrows that isolate them in unbreakable silos.

But leveraging is not only a question of transferring skills across levels and transforming competents into competence, it also concerns transforming knowledge into forms which allow the organisation to profit more effectively from it. Just as with many materials, any type of knowledge basically comes in three different forms: gas, fluid and solid. Gas is what we have in our minds. Fluid knowledge comes about when we discuss things with others. We know of a Swedish company called fluidminds that exploits this idea. And solid knowledge is the stuff that is embodied in customer offerings, routines and systems. In effect, a car, a PC, a software program, an ice-cream or whatever is in reality nothing more and nothing less than frozen creativity. We get an idea (gas); start discussing it with others (fluid); and finally develop a customer offering (solid).

The more solid the knowledge, the more money one can make. As we begin to freeze creativity, we also create opportunities for greater economies of scale. Take a consultant. Travelling around the world as a free agent he or she can probably make a pretty decent salary if loaded with fluid knowledge. But by writing a best-selling management book, or developing a management information system – freezing the knowledge – he or she can utilise the benefits of more or less costless reproduction.

Our science colleagues remind us that this is the triple point: in physics and chemistry, the *triple point* of a substance is the temperature and pressure at which three phases (gas, liquid, and solid) of that substance may coexist in thermodynamic equilibrium.

The problem with frozen creativity is that it is easy for our competitors to pick up a copy, take it to pieces and copy it. The icier it gets, the easier imitation becomes. And no longer can we put our trust in patents. We must rely on our ability to develop processes that enable us to deep-freeze new pieces of knowledge faster than the others – decreasing the duration of the insight-output cycle. The alternative is to bundle our frozen knowledge with more fluid or gas-like stuff – to sell provices and serducts. Think about GE, Xerox and IBM where the products are now little more than byproducts. The IT experts Gartner Group predicted that in 2003 services would represent 46 per cent of IBM's revenues. They were right and the figure is now over 50 per cent and, as we have noted, the company also sold off its PC business to Lenovo in China in 2004. But the real route to enhanced competitiveness is to combine and constantly bundle and re-bundle these different forms of knowledge – hyphenation.

How we create and leverage the knowledge of the firm are critically important questions. But increasing internal leverage does not mean creating a department for learning or knowledge management. Many companies in the West are now repeating the mistakes they made when realising that Japanese firms constantly beat them on quality. The answer then, as it seems to be now when knowledge is concerned, was to set up a department to handle the task. Quality was made into a big thing for a selected few, and we ended up with a bunch of quality engineers or managers running around trying to fix all the problems. Did it help? Not one bit. We must avoid making this mistake yet again. Instead, these responsibilities should be an integral part of everyone's job. Rather than knowledge management, the key to increasing internal leverage is knowledgeable management.

Industrial Leverage

Leverage is not only internal. With a clear focus on their key capabilities, funky organisations also use their core competencies and competents to enter new industries. But they do so without trying to control all processes internally.

Think back some 85 years. In the early twentieth century when Ford was founded, the company tried to control all inputs to the process. Since a car manufacturer used metals, you needed mines. The tyres were made of rubber, so you invested in a rubber plantation. Ford became a conglomerate. It got obsessed with controlling all input materials necessary

Ford's move made sense in the info desert of the early twentieth century. Welcome to the info jungle. A place where old Henry would feel as comfy as David Beckham with a ping-pong bat in his hand.

to make the product, rather than thinking about how its key capabilities could be leveraged into other areas.

The new logic means sticking to your competence, but utilising these skills in more than one industry. Today, we see at least three different types of industrial leverage.

First, there is *attitude-based* leverage. Having understood the needs of and targeted a specific tribe, the organisation may then use the fit in attitude to supply this tribe with more stuff. But it needs to convey the same vibe. The rap and hip-hop group the Beastie Boys, for instance, not only offers its tribe CDs and concerts, but magazines, T-shirts and a radio station as well. Similarly, rap star PDiddy (Sean Combs) and British group Underworld offer their own lines of designer clothing. They follow the tribe.

Second, many firms engage in *brand-based* leverage. Marlboro does it. Coca-Cola does it. Disney does it as a publishing, retailing and theme park operating company. Consider Richard Branson's Virgin which is involved in everything from airlines and railways to clothing and cosmetics and from pensions to Internet services. The organisation slavishly applies the core values of the brand when deciding whether or not to enter a new industry. At Virgin a new customer offering must be:

- of the best quality;

- innovative;

- good value for money;

- challenging to the existing alternatives; and

- add a sense of fun or cheekiness.

Virgin's management says that as many as 90 per cent of the projects it studies are, at least potentially, extremely profitable, but if a fit to these values cannot be found, they are rejected. Branson and his colleagues understand that a brand is more than a name or a logo – it is a promise and a contract with each and every customer with whom you are dealing. And if people feel that the offering does not live up to what they expect from the brand, they may well decide to stop buying the other stuff as well.

Third, there are lots of cases of more purely *competence-based* leverage. Honda focuses on engines, but utilises its knowledge to make cars, motorcycles and so on. 3M is an expert on adhesives. The Japanese company KAO is a major player in the branded packaged goods industry – nappies, shampoos, lotions, etc. A couple of years ago it was also one of the largest producers of floppy-discs. Lotions and floppy-discs? Well, if you believe that you are an expert in minimising friction, maybe the logic isn't that strange. Or look at AT&T which considers itself an excellent processor of transactions. It has a great brand and customer relationships characterised by permanence and trust. Put all this together and the company's move into the credit card business can be understood.

International Leverage

No surprises, leverage needs also to be international. Funky Inc. is a global corporation. But global does not necessarily mean big. Midget multinationals – like *Legshow* – are already all around us. The next time you go to the dentist, ask if you can keep the slurp, the disposable saliva sucker. Take a look at it. There is a 50 per cent chance that it comes from a division within the Swedish company Bergman & Beving. This unit holds a 50 per cent global market share in the slurp industry. How many employees does it have? It has less than 2,000. If you are one of 2,000 people at a company with a 50 per cent worldwide market share, you can really feel that you work in an international organisation. Do all the hundreds of thousands of employees at Siemens feel that way?

While globalisation is here, it is often not readily recognised in the organisation of firms. Although most companies *access* global markets through exports, and many have their *assets* internationally

In 2006 Kentucky Fried Chicken (KFC) opened more new restaurants in China than in the US.

dispersed in the form of foreign subsidiaries, few have managed to build global *administrative* structures and systems.

We also see clear differences across geography. To the typical US multinational, foreign usually equals marginal. Well-known international companies such as Microsoft and Intel still generate more than 70 per cent of their profits at home. At many US firms, non-US business is still relegated to a box in the organisational chart called RoW (Rest of the World). At the traditional Japanese multinational, foreign equals different. Critical decisions are mostly taken in Japan, by the Japanese.

The size of each territory shows the relative proportion of the world's population living there

But for many European multinationals, and particularly those from small countries such as Sweden, Finland, Holland and Switzerland, foreign has always equalled 'most of it' (MOI). Early on, these companies had to come up with ways and solutions to tackle global challenges. The result is usually that the role of headquarters is not as pronounced. Headquarters became the place where the mail was delivered. Now it may be even more narrow – the place where we by law are forced to hold the shareholders' meeting and where the CEO gets his or her business cards printed. These companies have many global centres of different kinds dispersed throughout the world. So if you want to learn more about managing across borders, look to European firms such as Philips, Electrolux, Nokia, Heineken, Unilever, TetraPak and Nestlé, rather than Wal-Mart or Mitsubishi.

And then there is the fourth and most important stage of globalisation – *attitudes*. No company we have ever come across is truly global in attitude. Home-country standards are often applied relatively uniformly. Key persons usually come from the same country. Products are mostly developed at home with the requirements of the local market in mind. The typical multinational is still parochial and ethnocentric. Foreigners are often regarded as strange. Or, as the Dutch expert on cross-cultural management Fons Trompenaars puts it: 'Understanding culture still seems like a luxury item to most managers.' Letting one of these managers loose in another culture is like inviting an elephant to dance in a china store.

Yet, only when we have become truly global in attitude can we reap all the other benefits of funkiness. To succeed, we need to move from conflict to reconciliation. We're not saying that it is easy to work in a global organisation. Differences in culture and languages and large geographical distances provide demanding challenges. There will be disagreements and misunderstandings aplenty. A few years ago a successful European MNC we worked with was given two prestigious awards for promoting equality between sexes. Before being presented with the awards, the CEO wanted to know exactly how equal the company was, in case someone asked. So, he sent a fax (remember that machine in the closet behind the copying machine) to all the subsidiaries asking for a report on the composition of the top management team broken down by sex. After two hours he received the first response. It was from the Finnish subsidiary: 'Dear Mr President, we have no one in the top-management team broken down by sex. However, we have one alcoholic.' Globalisation may be seen by many as a necessary evil, but that does not make it less essential.

FUNKY INC. IS INNOVATIVE

Funky Inc. is extremely innovative. In a real-time, globally linked surplus society it is just a matter of a few weeks, days or even hours before our friends from Bangalore, New York, Kuala Lumpur, Paris, Gdansk, Tokyo, Seoul, London or Santiago come here to copy our recipes. To remain unique, we must constantly sharpen our competitive edge. Venture capitalist Alan F. Shugart, former chairman of disk drive giant Seagate Technology Inc., goes as far to say that, 'Sometimes I think we'll see the day when you introduce a product in the morning and announce its end of life at the end of the day.' And IT guru Kevin Kelly says, 'Wealth flows directly from innovation... not optimisation... wealth is not gained by perfecting the known.'

By innovation we do not mean a dedicated department, a carefully fenced-off group of boffins. We mean total innovation – a frame of mind that applies to everyone at the company, everything, everywhere, and that goes on non-stop. It turns the company into an idea and dream factory that competes on imagination, inspiration, ingenuity and initiative.

If you think we are getting over-excited, think of an ordinary company selling some pretty dull products. Think of Rubbermaid which has been repeatedly selected by *Fortune* magazine as America's most admired corporation. This firm thrives on developing and producing plastic products such as buckets, dish-brushes and wastepaper baskets. To an uninspiring roster of products, Rubbermaid brings total innovation, imaginative zeal that converts the banal into something different and exciting. We draw the line at calling a bucket a sexy product.

Innovation permeates Rubbermaid. Some time ago the management team visited the British Museum in London. They left the building with a bunch of new ideas for kitchen products. Apparently, the ancient Egyptians knew things we have forgotten. Rubbermaid pillaged the ancient past with pride and considerable gusto. If Rubbermaid can do it, so can you. Innovation is rewarded in every industry.

Innovation is not only a matter of technology – nuts and bolts. In fact, technology is often only a small part of it. Innovation concerns every little aspect of how an organisation operates – administrative innovations, marketing innovations, financial innovations, design innovations, HRM innovations and service concept innovations. Going for total innovation, therefore, requires rethinking every little aspect of how we operate. This means reinventing strategy, increasing speed and thriving on smartness. But above all, total innovation requires ignoring *and* listening to the customers, as well as promoting internal heterogeneity *and* homogeneity – moving from a world of focusing on either or to one of achieving both, simultaneously. We are not talking about striking a balance – Funky Inc. combines extremes rather than settling for average solutions.

Innovate Through Reinventing Strategy

In a world where technology, institutions and values are in a state of turmoil, innovation is about rethinking what we are doing and about reinventing our industry. The US company Taco Bell, part of Pepsi Co., sells 'tex-mex' junk food. At one time, the company firmly believed that it was a player in the fast-food industry, and that the key to success was to increase market share, particularly in relation to other tex-mex restaurants. Reviewing the strategy, management realised that Taco Bell was really in the business of feeding people. The more challenging goal was to go for an increased share of stomach. In one second, the size of the market exploded from $70 billion to $550 billion. In five years, sales more than doubled. How? Well, if you are in the business of feeding people you better go out looking for the customers, rather than just expecting them to find you. So, Taco Bell set up

Redefine your industry so that your market share is cut to half of what it is today: then start to think about how to grow.

small, often portable restaurants at schools, hospitals, train stations, airports, libraries and other such places.

During the past few years, we have seen companies such as Dell, Amazon, Nike and Starbucks doing the same thing. They change the rules of the game. The uniqueness of these firms often rests with the soft and intangible aspects of their customer offerings rather than technology. Nike shifted its focus from being a shoe company to being a sports company. And then it shifted the focus from sports products as such to sporting performance and the superstars of sports. While most people don't talk about the characteristics of a particular tennis shoe or a golf putter, many are willing to dissect the performances of Roger Federer or Tiger Woods from every angle.

Howard Schultz, 'the espresso evangelist', and Starbucks took on the Herculean task of educating the American consumer about the fine coffees of the world. Contrary to what many would have expected, the company turned out anything but a modern age Sisyphus. The main advertising instruments were the local coffee shops where so-called baristas (bartenders) were trying to promote a lifestyle. And entering alliances with Barnes & Noble, Costco, United Airlines and others expanded this network.

There is nothing new about strategic innovation. In 1920, Ford had a 60 per cent market share in the US automotive industry. It churned out one new, shiny black Model T per minute. General Motors had to settle for a paltry 12 per cent of the market. Then, the legendary GM chief Alfred P. Sloan entered the stage. He reorganised the company into a multidivisional firm. The new strategic objective was a car 'for every purse and every purpose'. Three out of eight existing models were killed, and the remaining brands (Chevrolet, Oldsmobile, Pontiac, Buick and Cadillac) were each targeted at a particular segment of the market – and they came in more than one colour. Henry Ford had to close down his Dearborn factory for a year.

Innovate Through Speed

Not only does a larger geographical market necessitate a sharper focus, it also decreases the time available to exploit our capabilities. In a real-time society, getting faster to the future is obviously important. Funky Inc. operates in a world in which things are moving at a pace never before witnessed. No wonder that Gordon Forward, CEO of Chaparral Steel, concludes that, 'To stand still is to fall behind.' Once we have a clear focus on our core competencies, we need to act at the speed of light.

Velocity is a function of mass and energy. If your organisation has already de-massified by means of outsourcing, take the next step to speed things up be re-energising the corporation.

Traditionally, many European companies have been successful in what is usually referred to as mature industries. After you have erased the word synergy, please erase the word mature from your vocabulary and replace it with tired. We should no longer talk about mature industries or markets, but tired ones. Tired industries and markets are waiting for someone to do something revolutionary, radical and interesting. If we are entering a real time economy, a remote-control reality, people will zap to another company the instant they find that you are old, boring and out of date. Success is increasingly a question of being the leader of the pack, not a dedicated follower of fashion.

Innovate Through Smartness

Working faster is of course not a question of trying harder – just try doing the wrong things twice as fast – it is a matter of working smarter. Even though the current economy comes without speed limits, creativity cannot be forced upon people. To be creative we need slack. We need resources and time. We need time to sit down and reflect. We need time alone. We need time to play around. We need time to experiment. We need time to have casual conversations with others. In Japan, people sometimes refer to 'nommunication', rather than communication. Nommu is Japanese for drinking – and for once we are not talking about Coke. The time spent together in a bar after office-hours can be critical to the development of new ideas. A lot of venturing, mingling, socialising and relationship building in Silicon Valley is done in bars. So if thinking is working, put your feet back on the table, then leave the office and have a beer with your colleagues. Cut yourself some slack.

In a knowledge-based society, brains will always beat brawn. We all know that. But just how much of a company's intellectual capital is really used? If your organisation is normal, and by God we hope it's not, the answers usually range from 5 to 15 per cent. What would happen if a plant manager utilised only 5 to 15 per cent of existing manufacturing capacity? This person would be replaced in months or even weeks. This is apparently not the case when knowledge is concerned. The company's most critical asset is massively underutilised. Little wonder that people usually seem a bit embarrassed when this subject comes up – but they do tend to comply. Maybe 15 per cent isn't that bad after all? The only possible explanation is that somewhere along the line someone tricked us. They tricked us into believing that employment in reality only means 'competence castration'. As soon as we enter our office, the factory floor, or whatever, only 15 per cent of our body is supposed to be present – let's hope it's the upper 15 per cent.

We need whole persons – head and heart, body and soul. As it stands today, many organisations do not use knowledge – they abuse it. Something can be done and must be done. Remember what creativity expert John Kao says, 'Creativity is not like the weather – you can do something about it.' And no one can have a monopoly on creativity – not even a momentary one – not even Microsoft or Google.

Ignoring and Listening to Customers

Contrary to popular belief, getting to know customer requirements is not very difficult. Let us tell you what all customers want. Any customer, in any industry, in any market wants stuff that is both cheaper and better, and they want it yesterday. Organisations may spend millions of dollars every year getting McKinsey, Boston Consulting Group or A.T. Kearney to help them answer this question. But the simple truth is that the typical customer will always ask for improvements within the present frame.

Radical innovation in a discontinuous world means forgetting about forecasting and listening to marketing studies. Of course, history is littered with people who ignored customers and paid the price. Still, listening to the wrong customers, or listening without thinking, can be real killers as well.

Do you remember McLean, the low-fat hamburger from McDonald's? The product was introduced in response to the increased health-consciousness of the American consumer. The marketing tests revealed that it tasted almost as good as a Big Mac, but then no one ordered it. What did the company forget? Well, most people who enter a McDonald's restaurant are not health fanatics. The health-conscious eat elsewhere. The average McDonald's consumer is more interested in McLard than McLean.

A friend told us of being on a bus in the United States. The movie for the journey was _Super Size Me_, the engaging tale of living on McDonald's meals for a few weeks. Having sat through 90 minutes of depression about the effects of the company's food on people who consume a lot of it, the bus came to a routine stop. Handily located next to the stop was a McDonald's. Big Macs were ordered as if the movie had never been watched.

The reality is that we use and enjoy products that we wouldn't have wanted if they had been proposed to us at the very start of their development. A fax? If I am in a hurry I will use the phone, otherwise I will send a letter. A DVD? If it's on TV I want to watch it live, and if it's a movie I want to go to the theatre. CNN? More news, and in English? No thanks. Yet we all know what happened. We cannot expect the customer to think the unthinkable. That is our task. The responsibility for innovation always rests with the supplier. We must have the gifts and guts to imagine and work wonders. All this implies risk – total risk – and, at the end of the day, personal risk.

Read our lips. You cannot expect the customer to think the unthinkable. You may well think of yourself as a demanding and sophisticated customer. You may well be right. But would you have imagined that there could be a market for a tiny electrical chicken which requires regular feeding, nurturing and entertainment otherwise it dies? Yet the Tamagotchi – the tiny pet from cyberspace – was one of the great success stories of recent years.

Gallery visitors did not tell Picasso to invent cubism. Jazz fanatics did not suggest that Miles Davies should work with hip-hoppers. Moviegoers did not propose to Lars von Trier, the Danish film director, that he make *Breaking the Waves*. And customers sure as hell did not come up with the idea for CDNOW or Amazon.com. If you want to do something really interesting and revolutionary, learn to ignore your customers. Most customers function as rearview mirrors. They are extremely conservative and boring, lack imagination, and don't know their own minds. If customers are constantly beating you to new ideas, hire them or get another job.

Does technology-push really work? Just look at the US biotech company Amgen. It has been among the top performers on the *Fortune 1000* in terms of profitability for the past 10 years. The business concept of Amgen is to take brilliant science and find a use for it. It may well be that if customers don't like your solutions, they have the wrong problems. Unfortunately, in an age of abundance where the customers are in charge of the remote control, this is more problematic for you than for them.

If you are really innovative, you are also in a position to fire some of your customers. Many companies lose money on at least 50 per cent of their customers. Trouble is, most companies do not have a clue about who these customers are. Clearly, the risks associated with voluntarily or involuntarily firing the wrong customers are immense. For Ford a one per cent increase in customer loyalty is worth approximately $100 million per year in profits. When an unhappy customer walks out the door, how much money does your organisation lose if he or she decides never to come back? It could be $500, $5,000, perhaps even $50,000.

Paradoxically, Funky Inc. must also be extremely customised. We have to choose. Sometimes we must ignore the customer and do something radical and revolutionary, and in certain cases we must look upon the customer as a part of the firm and include them in value creation processes. In the

Customisation is not variation. Customisation is prosumption – providing the customer with a platform that enables him or her to co-design a limited edition product or service.

age of the demanding customer, it is no longer enough to produce slides and slogans saying that the customer is king.

Customise, then do it some more. 3M's Post-it notes now come in 18 colours, 27 sizes, 56 shapes and 20 fragrances. All in all, more than half a million combinations are available. The modularised trucks of SCANIA allow you to build your personal truck – cafeteria style. Or why not build your own doll, your own cuddly toy, your own Mr Potatohead? Barbie now comes complete with 15,000 combinations. The management gurus were right. Mass customisation is child's play. Change the outfit, the eyes, the colour, the hairdo, the clothes, the name – but don't even think about the legs. All for $40 (double the usual price). To get the customised doll, you need to fill out a questionnaire. Anne Parducci, VP of Barbie's owner Mattel, claims that the aim is to 'build a database of children's names, to develop a one-to-one relationship with these girls'. George Orwell eat your heart out, 1984 is here (a little late perhaps). And what do you think is valuable at Mattel – hundreds of kilos of doll-atoms or the brand and the database? Bits rule.

In a fragmenting world, niches are becoming ever smaller. Increasing individualisation combined with changes in technologies and values mean that micro markets have overtaken mass markets. The tail is long and lengthening. The next step is one-to-one manufacturing, one-to-one marketing, one-to-one everything, one customer–one solution. It is happening in industry after industry. We are entering a one-to-one society. Look at yourself in the mirror and staring back at you is the average size of a market segment in a surplus society. The new logic of the demanding customer is really simple. It is up to you to satisfy me, and I am not like you, you, or you.

Customisation can occur in all aspects of the customer offering; customised products, customised prices, customised opening-hours, customised promotion, etc. Total customisation. Tele-operators and utility companies let us design our own profiles for pricing and paying bills. MTV targets programming and commercials for different regions in Europe.

The recent developments in production equipment open up many new opportunities. We can move from mass production to flexible production and now mass customisation. With fewer tools we can produce more and better-quality models.

Customisation is also about your share of time. When and for how long are you prepared to do business with your clients? In an age of abundance, the customer decides when you can do business with him or her, not the opposite. Your only chance of survival is to move closer towards becoming a true 24-hour company – like Progressive Corp.

In addition, in some situations certain customers are your best consultants (and, always, the cheapest). The modern manager has one great advantage. Customers and employees have never been as smart as they are right now. The sensible executive treats them as assets, not assholes. A natural solution is to move power close to those people directly involved with the customers on a daily basis. Those engaged in the moment of truth activities, as former Scandinavian Airline Systems president Jan Carlzon put it, must be given the means to master the situation.

'Anything you can digitize, you can customize,' says Joseph Pine, author of *Mass Customization*. More or less everything is being customised.

You may not care that much for customised jeans or customised bed sheets. Each funky firm is not for everyone. We are talking super specialisation and ferocious focusing. And some will pay for it – though customisation is not necessarily more expensive. Car rental company Hertz discovered that by doing *only* what each customer actually required, its Gold service was in fact less expensive to provide than its Standard service.

Combining Heterogeneity and Homogeneity

Making radical changes possible calls for a much more personalised company. Oscar Wilde was right when he noted that, 'Consistency is the last refuge of the unimaginative.' Funky Inc. thrives on variation, difference and diversity. Funky Inc. welcomes people who are prepared to challenge the status quo, and to break with existing norms and regulations. Funky Inc. refuses to take part in the look-alike game anymore. No karaoke here.

Quite often people talk favourably about diversity since it supposedly promotes a better atmosphere and equality. Though arguments alluding to the 'fun and fair' consequences of increased variation may seem nice and laudable, this is not the stuff that convinces the typical manager to change the mix of people at the company. Instead, let us give you three solid economic reasons why heterogeneity pays.

1 Because $C = D^2$, where C stands for creativity and D for diversity. Lack of diversity often results in groupthink and intellectual constipation. We all know what the others think, so what's the use in talking to them? From the point of view of innovation, opposites attract. Novelty is the result of constructive misfits and tension. Cacophony Inc. replaces calamity with creativity.

2 More diversity generally decreases the average performance of a system but it also increases the standard deviation. The problem for Consistency Inc. is that in a world where the winner takes all, we do not compete on averages – we compete on exceptions. A firm with a lower average may well slaughter a rival with a higher average if the latter organisation lacks unique ideas that totally deviate from the norm.

3 To ensure success, the complexity of our environment must be reflected in the composition of the firm. Most academics refer to this as the Law of Requisite Variety. In practice, this means that when suppliers are from outside the home country of the organisation this must be reflected in the make-up of the organisation. If many of our customers are immigrants, this too must be reflected. If we deal with really young or old people this must be reflected. If we increasingly do business with women, this must be reflected. Eve-olution!

Unfortunately, many firms are so inbred that you sometimes expect the next person to walk through the door with an oversized head, red curly hair, and an extra eye in the middle of their forehead. Some organisations are like the

There is no point in winning the Star Wars if the sequel is called the *Rise of the Clones*.

Amish people. All people look the same and think that they can freeze time. Don't expect too much innovation at companies where 90 per cent of the employees are the same gender, about the same age, have a similar educational background, dress the same way, and all play golf. Even if they go on annual strategy conferences to the Mediterranean or the Alps to be really creative, wild and crazy, don't expect a great deal. A company with a board filled with white, male, 55-year-old Finns is unlikely to come up with an idea that is even slightly appealing to a young, coloured, female, lesbian, non-Scandinavian Muslim. Are the men on the board going to recruit Muslim lesbians? Of course not. Are all your managers cut from the same cloth?

Perhaps the guy in the picture should be the next CEO of your company. Maybe he holds the knowledge that could make you unique in the twenty-first century. But, would you, under any circumstances, hire this person? And, more to the point, would this individual, under any circumstances, apply for a position with your company? The man in the picture is Virgin-owner Richard Branson.

What if you are continually turning down applications from Anders Borg types? Or even worse, maybe these guys have stopped sending their CVs to you because they know that you care about how people look, dress, the colour of their skin, and so on.

We are not suggesting that you should start recruiting all the pony-tailed executives in the world, but simply that you have to be prepared for the consequences of developing a brain-based firm. And allowing people to be themselves and to look as they want appears a fundamental starting point.

The competitive reality is that organisations that are bogged down in issues of race, gender, age, sexual preferences, looks and so on will slip deeper down in the mire. They will encounter serious problems when competition moves softwhere. Intelligence is normally distributed. It is not the preserve of white, 45-year-old males.

As Michael McNeal, director of corporate employment at Cisco Systems, pointed out: 'If you want to find great people you've got to look in unusual places.' Recruiting only from Harvard Business School or INSEAD in France will result in a pretty homogeneous crowd. Instead, Cisco tries to find people at the Boston Marathon and the Mountain View International Microbrewery Festival.

Admittedly, an entire company of Richard Branson or Peter Lewis types would be quite difficult to manage. We are not saying that you should move from hierarchy to anarchy. Instead, we are simply suggesting that sharing a number of things will be helpful. What can you share? The choice is endless. How about shared ownership, rewards, identity, culture, language, knowledge and attitudes?

Stock options for all employees. Marx meets the Wild Capitalist West. Shared ownership is increasing everywhere. At GE more than 35,000 employees are currently given stock options, as compared to merely 200 during the 1980s. In 1996, the Bean Stock programme at Starbucks coffee shops allowed employees who joined the firm in 1991 to cash in options for $50,000. Fat bonuses are no longer necessarily the privilege of a select few. Power to the people. Remember that most software companies were incorporated to share ownership and wealth, not to raise capital. And we ain't seen nothin' yet.

Funky Inc. is neither homogeneous nor heterogeneous; it is *both*. Successful companies will evolve into organisational tribes – biographical organisational tribes. And in a tribe people get the energy from one another. The Zulus have a word for it: 'ubuntu' (short for *unmunta ngumuntu nagabuntu*). This can be translated, a person is a person because of other persons. Or as Carl Jung put it, 'I need we to be fully I.'

Let us ask you a personal question. Do you regularly visit gay clubs? Let's be honest now. Well, if you do, as a man you are struck by a number of things. No. 1 – there's a lot of men in here. No. 2 – they're all so different – some are old, others young, some nurses, others business managers, students, doctors,

Tribal gathering

everything that you could ever think of. The only thing these people have in common is their sexual orientation. By keeping one thing constant we allow for variation in all other dimensions.

At McKinsey and several other consulting firms, all the employees have at least one thing in common. They are insecure overachievers. This is a way of keeping people together and assuring some continuity in an otherwise discontinuous world. At Quad Graphics blood or marriage at one time related more than 50 per cent of the 8,500 or so employees. Once, someone even said that the Mafia gets more resignations than a company such as 3M with its extremely strong culture. Have you thought of, identified and worked with the lowest common denominator of your organisation?

And just how do you get people to share your values? Short answer: find those who already do. Look at Hell's Angels or Greenpeace. 'We hire attitudes,' says Herb Kelleher of SouthWest Airlines. The logic is that you can make positive people into good pilots, but turning great pilots with attitude problems into charming servers of customers is close to impossible. Funky Inc. recruits people with the right attitude, then it trains them in skill – not the reverse. We can no longer bring in smart people and then brainwash them at training camps. Ideally, of course, we try to attract people that are smart *and* share our values. But, if you are forced to choose, go for attitude. Lenin was right again. Find the revolutionaries. Do not try to change people.

The tribe is not necessarily restricted to the legal boundaries of the firm. Look at Harley-Davidson. By inviting the consumer tribe it has targeted to join the organisational tribe, the firm has dramatically extended its community. It uses parties to initiate new members. Storytelling around the campfire keeps the messages moving throughout the tribe. Closing ceremonies and continuous reinforcement are also part of the deal. What Harley-Davidson and other Funky Incs. have realised is that a tribe targeting another tribe does not merely have to produce value – the customers also want values.

FUNKY INC. IS HETERARCHICAL

A Greek called Dionysius the Aeropagite introduced the concept of hierarchy some 1,500 years ago. The word literally means 'to rule through the sacred'. Now, Dionysius was not the mythological wine lover. He was scholastic rather than alcoholic; interested in God and the Devil, in heaven and hell. Somehow, Dionysius figured out that heaven is (was?) hierarchically organised. Not only that, he also argued that this celestial structure had exactly nine levels with God as the CEO, the archangels making up the top management team, and Jesus Christ in a staff position to the right of God. If you fear that you may not end up in this place, do not worry. According to the Aeropagite, hell is also hierarchically organised – with nine layers. One might suspect that the entire structure is turned upside down, however, with purgatory as the prime motivator to 'climb' the ladder.

Hierarchy builds on three key assumptions: your environment is *stable*, your processes are *predictable*, and your output is *given*. You know where you are, what you do, and what will happen – the same competitors, customers, suppliers, technologies and product offerings – year in and year out. As long as this holds true, it is utterly stupid to organise in any other way. However, we seriously doubt that you would use any of those three words to describe your reality. And in a surplus society, an economy moving forward at turbo speed, and in companies heavily reliant on brain power, traditional hierarchies will get constant nervous breakdowns.

The enemies of hierarchy:
Internationalisation causes dispersion of corporate competencies.
Hyphenation leads to diversity.
Education increases depth.
Innovation diminishes durability.

Since hierarchy assumes that the sources underlying competitive advantage are given and eternal, the organisational challenge is to find a structure that will be an efficient exploiter of this specific combination of knowledge. So, we developed organisational structures that excelled in spitting out yet another standardised customer offering. But in an age of abundance with total global competition, overcapacity in more and more industries and increasingly powerful customers, we need to be different. We need innovation and renewal of our recipe. We need structures that support experimentation and the creation of novelty.

Funky Inc. applies organisational solutions capable of combining and recombining knowledge across any type of border at the speed of light. And hierarchy simply is not for hyphenation and combination, it is for separation and division. So forget organisational pyramids with the CEO sitting atop. Who wants to work in pyramids, the greatest tombs ever created by man? Playgrounds must gradually replace the pyramids.

The Funky Model

The traditional hierarchical firm won't be a problem in the twenty-first century – it won't be around. The new organisation will be heterarchical – containing many hierarchies of different kinds.

In reality, all firms have three overlapping systems of positions, professions and processes. The positional structure

**The new leadership troika:
Position: Pope
Professional: Plato
Process: Patton.**

is a contact book with addresses and numbers. The professional structure tells you something about the skills of people, and the process structure shows you what is actually going on. Everyone can be included in all of these categories, but in different places. The positional structures are manifested in our organisational charts. The process structures are represented by boundary-spanning activities and projects. The professional structures are a lot more messy and dependent on the skills of individuals placed all over the landscape of the firm, and increasingly also outside the legal boundaries of the company.

Historically, we have made the mistake of only recognising the positional structure. Senior executives managed these structures, controlled all important processes and projects, and their professional knowledge was regarded as omnipotent. Many companies still make this mistake. The typical boss, no matter what type of organisation or formal position in the hierarchy, is obsessed with knowing and controlling everything. The basic assumption has been that since people are stupid, they can only handle really simple jobs so we better have super-complex organisational structures.

Today, we need to transform complexity into simplicity. Jack Welch goes as far as to call bureaucracy the Dracula of organisational design. No matter how much we fight it, bureaucracy always comes back to haunt us. So we have to keep putting sticks through its heart and garlic in our pockets.

In the face of an increasingly complex knowledge landscape we have to strengthen the power of the professional and process structures. Firms need stronger project leaders as well as intellectual champions with sufficient organisational clout. But neither of these structures should dominate totally. If action drives the entire system the result is ad-hocracy and, if we let knowledge be the single organising principle, the resulting structure is a meritocracy.

Total domination by one of the principles leads to bureau*crazy*, ad-ho*crazy* and merito*crazy*, rather than anything else. All three aspects of the modern firm need to exist simultaneously – in our minds. And the latter point is critically important. The funky model is not a three-dimensional matrix. We will not solve problems by simply rearranging the boxes and arrows. It is a frame of mind, a philosophy. And we are not talking about a topless organisation. The alternative to hierarchy is not *no-archy*. There is still a critical role for management to play. But they are no longer the only actors or stars.

Seven Features of the Funky Firm

So how will Funky Inc. work? Well, let us provide you with seven principles for organising the firm. Some you will recognise, but the real trick is getting them all to work together in harmony.

1 Smaller

Throughout the twentieth century the predominant corporate myth was that big was good. From Henry Ford to Michael Eisner, Alfred P. Sloan to Jack Welch, size has been considered all-important. Bravado, of a peculiarly male kind, has dominated. The current fashion for bigger and bigger mergers is just the latest manifestation of this obsession. We may accept that quantity is not quality in virtually every other area of life, but in business organisations the two remain hopelessly intertwined and confused.

Now, those that are large are no longer in charge. In the mid-1970s, *Fortune 500* companies employed 20 per cent of the US workforce. Today, that figure is less than 9 per cent. Similarly, companies with fewer than 19 employees account for 29 per cent of US exports – in comparison it has been estimated that the *Fortune 500* generates a mere 7 per cent.

Funky Inc. is small because, as pointed out by American commentator George Gilder, 'The smaller the space; the larger the room.' We are creative in small teams. Maybe the inhabitants of the Stone Age can teach us something. Back then, the average number of people in a tribe was some 40 individuals. On the African Savannah Plain 200,000 years ago, clans appeared to have had a maximum of around 150 members. Nigel Nicholson of London Business School points to 'the persistent strength of small to midsize family businesses throughout history. These companies, typically having no more than 150 members, remain the predominant model the world over, accounting for approximately 60 per cent of all employment'.

The optimum size of a company is a matter of perennial debate. Virgin chief Richard Branson argues that 50 to 60 people is enough. 'If a company gets too large, break it into smaller parts. Once people start not knowing the people in the building and it starts to become impersonal, it's time to break up a company,' he says. Bill Gates claims that around 200 is the maximum. Nathan Myhrvold, then R&D manager at Microsoft, said that eight people is about enough.

2 ■ Flatter

The funky firm is flatter. Flatter so that the time from problem detection to solution implementation is reduced. The need to flatten the firm is hardly big news to any of you, but this might be. There are two very different ways of making a company flatter. The first is to take a sledgehammer and hit the organisation on the top while simultaneously raising the lower levels by means of training and education. The second way is to take your hand, reach into the centre of the organisation and tear out the middle.

In the West we have had a preference for this second type of solution – getting rid of the middle. We all know how 'boring and conservative' middle managers are. Now, we believe there is an inherent danger to this. We may end up relying on 'seniles' managing 'juveniles'. Our experience is that often the best and most critical people sit in the middle. We only have to use them in the right way – as a value-adding link between the top and the bottom; translating vision into action and action into vision. Many Japanese companies no longer talk about bottom-up or top-down processes. Instead, they realise that real organisational action is dependent on processes better characterised as middle-up-down.

3 ✂ Temporary

Funky Inc. is temporary. By this we refer to working in projects and groups. Most of us know that teams are what Ed Lawler at the University of Southern California calls the Ferraris of organisational design. They are high performance, but also high maintenance and incredibly expensive. Still, the changing circumstances of today's business world do not allow us to use one stable, unisex, one-size-fits-all structure. We have to be able to recombine our key assets and turn the firm into a team-park. To succeed, we need to institute a culture which mixes aspects of daring and sharing.

One of the principal problems relates to the fact that people will have to become used to no longer having a job. At funky firms people have many jobs. Today, the woman in the room next to you is your boss – tomorrow you are hers. Our careers are becoming more like those of actors. In the morning you are playing Macbeth, and later that day you are the Terminator or Lara Croft. Naturally, this will cause serious problems for those who find security in having a piece of paper saying 'job description' at the top. The new reality gives these people nightmares of Ingmar Bergman-ish proportions. One of the key tasks for leaders is to help people find themselves at ease and enjoy this new situation.

4   Horizontal

Funky firms work horizontally, in processes. The vertical hierarchical logic builds upon the simple assumption that the smart ones are located at the top and the stupid ones at the bottom. Hierarchy divides people into those that think and those that merely do. In reality, however, we know that most opportunities and problems in a company occur horizontally – across functions, business areas, divisions or countries. Moreover, there is little room for suppliers and customers in a vertical logic – they sit outside the firm.

As long as the preferred strategy was addition, through acquisitions, mergers and diversification, the natural principle for structuring the firm was that of division. However, when the hallmark of a competitive strategy shifts to subtraction, through focusing and outsourcing, the preferred structural denominator should be multiplication – combining stuff from different parts of the network into new customer offerings. This is just simple management by metrics. If the main aim is to build an organisation where the whole is greater than the sum of the parts, division is a highly inefficient method.

5 Circular

All really fast systems, such as our brain, use circular design. This principle is perhaps more difficult to grasp. It builds on the fact that we have a tremendous ability to self-organise once we get 360-degree feedback. Circularity is about organisational democracy. At your company, who appoints the CEO? The board, of course. Well, in most organisations marked by knowledge intensity this is the task of the other members of the firm. The other professors mostly elect the dean at a university. The other partners appoint the head at McKinsey and at most other consulting companies. This is also reflected in the shared ownership of the firm. The cardinals decide who becomes the pope in the Catholic Church. (Letting the board decide could be somewhat problematic in the latter case.)

6 🚪 Open

Unfortunately, simply changing internal structures won't suffice. Given that the firm is narrower and hollower, we also need to develop abilities to become increasingly networked. For Focused Inc. the future will mean more joint ventures, strategic alliances and partnerships. Not all assets can be kept internally. The network, rather than the single firm, is becoming the relevant unit of analysis and action. Cooperate with customers, suppliers *and* competitors. Corporate adultery becomes OK when you really need the skills and resources of a competitor. Business is not a zero-sum game. This calls for a new type of logic. As noted by Professor Robert Axelrod, 'In zero sum games you always try to hide your strategy but in non zero sum games you might want to announce your strategy in public so the other players need to adapt to it.'

7 ⛎ Measured

Control freaks of the world, do not despair. Control will not disappear. It will only become more indirect. We do not foresee that the main use of IT for a lot of organisations will lie in increasing communication, coordination, customisation and external contacts. Instead, information systems will be used to increase control by measuring more things, new things, at multiple levels, and at a greater frequency than before. To a certain extent, this is a substitute for the loss of hierarchical control resulting from the introduction of new structures.

How many firms really measure not only their own but also their customers' market and mindshare? Are these guys the fastest growing in their industries? How many companies systematically organise knowledge about their competitors and suppliers? How many firms measure things such as innovation, employee stuff, attractiveness, human exports, company demographics, environmental impact and so on? How many companies measure their return on knowledge (ROK), return on decency (ROD) or return on people (ROP)? And just who is responsible for measuring all these new things?

We need appropriate goals. The sophisticated companies of today use stretch goals, goals that challenge people to perform beyond what they thought was possible. Stretch goals are general. You do not tell the experts how to do it – you provide a challenging benchmark. Now, this is easier said than done. Not only are these goals hard to attain, it is also difficult to set them. It is difficult because we all have psychological limitations. Most of us know that the present way of doing things is not perfect, but we do believe that we are fairly close to the optimal solution. It is tricky to pose goals that almost seem ridiculous and unattainable.

Management thinker Charles Handy tells the story of Ford Motors which experienced exactly this problem when deciding to lay off 100 people at the accounts receivable department. People screamed 'We just about managed to do this with 500 employees, how are we supposed to manage with only 400?' It took some time, but finally the company had done it. Champagne bottles were opened and everyone was happy. Some time later the company launched a major benchmarking project, in which the goal was to study the Japanese competitor Mazda. The Ford people were surprised to find that

Mazda had only five employees in its equivalent department. Ford had to rethink its way of operating. Finally, it managed to come down from 400 employees to 100.

Why did Ford not set this goal from the beginning? The answer is psychological precincts. Such improvements seemed impossible within the existing paradigm. A lot of people would say that if you believe that you can do it with 100 persons, then you must have been pretty stupid using 500. For protection, we lock on a certain logic. To make real changes we have got to rethink our basic assumptions and break free from the logic of the past. We need what Konusuke Matsushita used to call, 'Torawarenai sunao-na kokoro' – a mind that does not stick.

A RECIPE FOR SUCCESS?

So you have focused, leveraged your competencies in all imaginable directions, created an innovative company that is anything but hierarchically organised. But are these changes adequate? Is this the recipe for future success? Short answer: NO! All the changes that we have proposed – all the traits of Funky Inc. – are merely necessary but not sufficient for securing future success. But they are necessary. Very necessary. The problem is that all companies are doing it. All organisations are refocusing, realigning, renewing, reorganising, re-engineering, etc.

The word competition comes from Latin and literally means 'seeking together' or 'choosing to run in the same race'. But in an age of abundance the tracks are pretty crowded. The others are constantly stepping on your toes, pushing and elbowing you, trying to get to the customers first. So, and slightly paradoxically, the only (un)reasonable thing to do is *not* to compete. As soon as we start running

Is your strategy focused on being better? If so, you have, as strategy guru Michael Porter puts it, bet on the stupidity of your competitors.

alongside all the others, in our pursuit of market share, mindshare, or whatever-share, we risk ending up as one in the crowd – invisible to the customers. When we take part in the same race for top talent as all the others it is hard for people to tell the difference.

The dirty little secret of market capitalism in all its many forms is that successful companies have become so by killing the spirit of free enterprise. They have all succeeded in creating monopolies, at least for a short moment in time. Competitiveness comes about by not competing. Success arises from being different, from not participating in the karaoke bar. And then being prepared to change again.

FUNKY U
5

*'We must be the change
we wish to see in the world'*
Mahatma Gandhi

Shopping and fucking.

Shopping and fucking are the only things left.

Shopping and fucking shape the dreams of our times.

Shopping and fucking, says controversial British playwright Mark Ravenhill, are the only things that really motivate the younger generation. Shopping and fucking are what really get their juices flowing.

Together with the statement that Karl Marx was right, this quote got us into more trouble than all other sentences in Funky Business combined. In the UK people referred to it as shopping & sex and then giggled nervously. The producer of a morning TV show in the US told us that we could talk about everything in the book except page 185. Apparently communism, commerce and copulation made us too hot to handle.

So, you might then ask, who are the leaders of these champions of retailing and copulation? In many cases, they are still middle-aged men who probably haven't had steaming sex since the late seventies and who leave the shopping to the rest of their family.

Over the top? Excessive? Perhaps. But, even if Mark Ravenhill is only 25 per cent right – indeed even if he is only 10 per cent right – we had better come up with new ways to organise our companies, new ways to capture the attention of

demanding customers, *and* new ways to treat our colleagues –
peers, bosses and subordinates. We have to motivate them in
new ways, find new ways to evaluate and reward them, train
them, inspire them and lead them. In the Funky Village, people
do not get their kicks from celibacy and savings.

Never forget or underestimate how strongly celibacy and
saving were enshrined in previous eras. In the Old World,
people saved, as they still do in Japan – the only country where
people have to be given money and told to go shopping –
because it was the route to betterment. Similarly, celibacy was
the route to spiritual improvement. These two pillars of the Old
World are crumbling. Leisure and pleasure are the new reality.
Instant gratification is expected. Fucking and shopping. Freud
and Jung (in that order) set loose.

One is right, one is dead

The legacy of self-motivation left by Martin Luther in Europe is now being cast off. The self-motivated employee used to wake up every morning eager to go to work – praying by working. Then, one day, he or she just decided to stay in bed. Today, people work to get rich, to have fun, to meet new people, see new places and be seen, to develop themselves, or whatever. But, they no longer work out of moral obligation. Work is no longer automatically accepted as a good thing. Motivation is no longer taken for granted. We've moved from *have to* to *want to*.

If you combine the fact that Martin Luther's tenets and assumptions are dead with the fact that Karl Marx was right, things take on a radically different appearance. Martin Luther is dead × Karl Marx was right = Mega-challenges for the modern manager (as well as society in general). Suddenly the organisation is – from the individual's perspective – disposable rather than permanent. Today, people hire organisations, rather than vice versa. Says former presidential adviser and Secretary of Labor Robert Reich, 'It is a seller's market for talent. People can afford to shop around for the right boss... the right environment. In the old economy it was a buyer's market... It was why hire? Now why join up?'

In the long run, Charles Handy claims that this also means that the main task of the company will no longer be to employ people, as it once was. The key task will be to organise. Clearly, there is a huge difference between being a great employer and a great organiser.

The organiser offers opportunities rather than jobs – a creative space. An organiser has to take an idea, identify the resources required to make it happen, then attract those resources. An inspired organiser can mobilise armies of intellectual mercenaries overnight to solve a specific problem.

In the organising paradigm, nothing is given. Tasks may change. It is temporary, a potent and unstable fusion of ideas and people. Risk, dynamism and constant value creation are the driving forces of organising. Leaders must create force fields – magnets that suck in talent, rather than having permanent employees sucking up to them.

The organising paradigm means that the legal boundaries of the firm are of less and less importance. It is the operational boundary that counts. The leader handles an array of partners and collaborators, network upon network. It's the United Firms of Unilever rather than Unilever. It's the United Firms of Nike rather than Nike. Inspiration must be provided to the extended family/the network and only the best will do. There is more: these individuals/firms have alternatives each and every minute of each and every day. People have to be treated like celebrities. They are Hollywood stars or sports stars, demanding prima donnas. Upset them at your peril. Lose one and they will all go. Stars attract stars; losers pull in losers. We are all players in the great global attraction game. Individuals are players. Companies are players and regions are players. Cities are certainly players. Look at London and its irresistible attractiveness to financial companies. At the end of the day – Silicon Valley is nothing more and nothing less than a pretty attractive place inhabited by some pretty attractive organisations and individuals.

In such a world, fundamentally different demands are imposed on leaders – and this applies to political and religious leaders as well as those in business. In fact, it applies to all leaders – Boy Scout leaders, sports coaches, directors, union representatives, and so on.

Our world has moved from *the Madonna* of the Bible to *'Lady Madonna'* of the Beatles to *Madonna* the iconic chameleon; from *we* to *I*. Express yourself! The new riff pulls us in improbable directions – Bollywood via the Buena Vista Social Club to Britney Spears. It is as individual as we are. As unique as DNA. Fingerprinting males and females. Whether they are Harry Potter creator J.K. Rowling, golfer Annika Sörenstam, Nelson Mandela, super-architects Frank Gehry and Shigeru Ban or even our old friend Bill Gates, individuals are shaping the world. After the collapse of communism, the rise and fall of dot-communism, and the sometimes violent questioning of capitalism, the dominant *ism* left on earth is individualism.

MEANINGFUL LEADERSHIP

Mobilising forces is no longer straightforward. People don't snap to attention. They don't passively fall into line. When power is in the hands of the people, intimidation and threats do not work. And, if they do work, you are dead because you hired the wrong people.

People are everything. Bill Gates still dedicates a lot of time to attracting the most talented people to Microsoft. There is nothing new in this – the best leaders have been spending time on recruitment for decades, if not centuries. King Arthur did it. Cosimo di Medici did it. Duke Ellington did it. Ronald Reagan did it.

Consider some of the key leadership tasks: *selection* (of people), *expectations* (defining goals), *motivation* (of employees) and *amplification* (making individuals grow). They all deal with people.

The word management comes from Italian 'maneggio/ maneggiare' and the French word 'manège', the training ring in which horses run around encouraged by a long whip held by the horse trainer. But what if the horses learned to run around by themselves? What if the horses actually do a better job at running around without the man, age 46.5, holding a whip and standing in the middle? Or, what if the horses have even figured out that in a surplus society with complete global competition there are probably more sensible things to do than to keep on running around in circles? If you try to break-in smart people, they will break-out.

People may no longer be so obedient, but that does not mean that leadership is redundant. On the contrary, the funky world requires limitless leadership. This will not involve our traditional notion of a leader. Not that traditional leaders ever really existed – real leaders exist only in the heads and hearts of those who believe in them.

The trouble is that modern management is often built on the assumption that the absence of leadership results in chaos. The nightmare is pyromaniac leadership in a firm inhabited by corporate arsonists constantly threatening the well-being of the company. In this nightmare, the task of the leader is simply to put out the fires. Top management team = Fire department.

We do not believe that putting out fires is the job of the leader. Nor is it the task of *the* leader to bring order to chaos. Take leadership away and you do not automatically get corporate chaos desperately in need of firm leadership. Take leadership away and you usually get repetition and reproduction. The organisation becomes constipated, incapable of self-renewal.

Instead, a major role of leaders, anywhere and everywhere, is to infuse chaos into order. Rather than hunting down pyromaniacs, we are talking about prophylactic leadership. The main aim is to make yourself abundant. Leaders = Midwives. Leaders must challenge people to depart from the patterns of the past and to destroy the present profit-makers by creating new ones. *Meaningful* leadership is about stirring the pot rather than putting on the lid. Funky leaders are creators of chaos as much as originators of order. It is the job of great leaders – not only *the* leader – to support the organisation in combining order and chaos.

From the point of view of those being led, a group to which we all belong at certain times, four critical requirements of funky leaders will arise: increased calls for direction and tolerance, attraction and attention.

Direction – Spin Me

Direction is not a matter of command and control, but of focusing, allowing and encouraging people to focus on what really matters. It is spiritual management rather than micro-management. In a chaotic world, people cry out for individuals who can provide MEANING to their private and professional lives. There remains a perpetual need for guidance. Guidance is manifested through formulating and clarifying underlying assumptions about the world, our capabilities and what we want to happen. These assumptions are the existential foundation of any business.

All organisations need a shared idea of why they exist, who they are, and where to go. In modern businesses this is usually expressed through a vision. The problem is that most companies do not have an operationally potent vision. Instead, most are generic wishlists whose length is matched only by their emptiness – *wishons*. Visions should be unique. They should differentiate.

In practice, visions often tend to be vacuums. People frequently tell us that the vision of their firm is to make money. But is this really unique? Do all their competitors focus on losing money? All visions should be able to survive a triviality test. If it sounds stupid when you negate it – our vision is not to make money – go back to square one and try again.

To provide direction, a vision should be clear, continuous and consistent. It should inspire commitment and be continually communicated. Funky leaders communicate, then communicate the same thing again, and again, and again. They never grow tired or, at least, never appear to grow tired.

Scott McNealy of Sun Microsystems has a favorite formula: 0.6L. Every time information passes a layer in the organisation only 60 per cent gets through. This quickly adds up – especially in hierarchical firms with an excessive number of layers. Once you have tried informing people the first time, maybe one per cent have got it. When you believe you have 90 per cent on board, perhaps 10 per cent are beginning to understand.

We need to over-inform not because people are stupid, but because people have other, more important things on their mind, such as their kids, vacation and the up-coming visit from their mother-in-law. Work matters but it is never the only thing. And if it is, once again, you should question if these rather one-dimensional obsessives are the right people for your business.

Truth be told, many managers need to over-inform because they have made such a bad job of communicating in the past that there is a huge reservoir of scepticism and cynicism directed at any talk of visions and missions. People know from experience that visions do not matter and that another will be along in a year or two.

With the onus on communication, leaders are spin-doctors. Their job is to be general *and* overly precise. It is an impossible paradox but one which they have to make possible. Essentially, they distil the company direction into the most potent capsule. At Disney the vision is to 'make people happy' and at Motorola it is 'Wireless'. 3M focuses on

Companies with a strong culture and a clear sense of values do not need a behavioural bible inspired by Stalin.

'solving unsolved problems'. AT&T talks about IM&M – 'information movement and management'. These statements are simple enough to be shared by all employees, and they are clear in saying what the companies should *not* be doing. Try showing up at Motorola with a wire and see what happens. Can you say this about your organisation's vision?

As well as visionary bullets, we also need more short-term-oriented goals that inspire change and that change over time. Jim Collins and Jerry Porras, in their book *Built to Last*, call such things big hairy audacious goals (BHAGs). These come in many shapes and forms. They can be quantitative or qualitative. In the early 1990s, US retailer Wal-Mart set its aim on 'becoming a $125 billion company by the year 2000'. In contrast, almost 100 years ago Ford decided to 'democratise the automobile'. BHAGs can be geared towards a common enemy such as Nike's 'Crush Adidas' from the 1960s, or they can use role models as a benchmark. In the 1940s Stanford University decided to try to 'become the Harvard of the West'. A more inwardly oriented focus was used by General Electric in its 1980s goal: 'Become number one or two in every market we serve and revolutionise this company to have the strengths of a big company combined with the agility of a small company.'

As well as being the distilled essence of what a company is and what a company stands for, visions and goals should also ignite and inspire commitment. People must want to belong. They must be banging on your door to sign up. Simply and powerfully, the International Red Cross is there 'to serve the most vulnerable'. Do you really feel a tingle or see tears in the eyes of your colleagues when you discuss your company's vision?

Communicating a vision not only involves repetition and a carefully distilled message; it demands the ability to tell a story. True leaders are CSOs – Chief Storytelling Officers. They provide the focus, inspiration and meaning that the organisation has been crying out for. Danish children's book author Hans Christian Andersen is probably, at times, more useful in the corporate trenches than the management prophet, the late Peter Drucker, father of modern management.

Metaphors and language are incredibly powerful. Indeed, language shapes and reshapes the world around us. It can reassure – words such as airport and Internet, for example, are combinations of old words used to describe new phenomena (a port for ships in the air?) – and it can help create a new world. Stories and myths contain a built-in tension that draws people in and ensures that the message sticks. They are adaptable, open to an array of interpretations, and are universal and eternal. They communicate more than mere facts.

Look at the major religious texts – the Bible, the Koran, Bhagavad-Gita, etc. They communicate wisdom through metaphors, stories and analogies. And when rules are used, they tend to be short and snappy. In the Old Testament, God tells Moses to apply a mere 10 commandments rather than a complex plethora of rules and regulations. The advice for the modern-day manager is to go for the generic – do not try to nail down all the specifics. Put your trust in the good judgement of people.

Funky leaders give rise to and spread stories. They communicate messages through the stories that they tell and which emerge around them. At IKEA, the company founder, Ingvar Kamprad, uses storytelling. For example, many know the story of Kamprad travelling by bus to and from airports to save money. It is a simple story, easily told in a single sentence, but its ramifications and its message are very powerful. Here is a rich man who is still in touch with reality, who is concerned with value, who is the same as us. Kamprad's bus journeys are a metaphor of the values

Successful leaders live the values of the company 24/7 and continually set the culture. Culture comes from the top.

A short story, indeed!

embodied by IKEA. The other thing about stories is that few care if they are true or not. Myths outweigh facts.

Applying management by stories also means that the leader is held to ransom by the organisation. Management by rules allows managers to use a set of differentiated and people-specific standards. It is OK for executives to travel business class, but those not part of the top management team still need to save money on paperclips. But when we communicate generic insights through stories the ramifications of divergent behaviour are great. Kamprad in a cab? No way. Nor can he order champagne and caviar; or stay at the Peninsula in Hong-Kong or the George V in Paris. He is condemned to stay at middle-ranking hotels and to ride on buses. Any champagne must be consumed behind closed curtains – and in a transparent society all curtains are made of cellophane.

The message is simple: light the campfire, gather the tribe and start preaching and practising. Lift us up where we belong.

Funky leaders give rise to and spread stories

Experimentation – Forgive Me

Business life has, until now, been built around spurts of creation and extended periods of exploitation. Companies exploited natural resources, exploited technologies and actually exploited people. We are good at exploitation because we have hundreds, not to say thousands, of years of experience. We know exactly what to do when we find a gold mine. We put structures and systems in place and get to work. When it is exhausted we look for the next gold mine.

In contrast, we are not very good at creation. Our societies are not built for it. Our organisations are not designed for it. Our schools are not made for it. And most people are not trained for it.

By its very nature, creation involves a departure from traditional structures and frames. In a world of creativity-sucking board meetings, past structures have ruled the roost. Now, we have to be prepared to depart from the agenda. Creativity also demands the introduction of some new structures. Creation is not, repeat not, anarchical.

Pursuing other routes than the one most travelled can prove worthwhile. Get off the beaten track. After all, Viagra was discovered when the scientists were looking to develop a drug to relieve high blood pressure; Columbus was actually trying to reach India rather than America; and Fleming's penicillin was the result of a 'failed' experiment, as was galvanised rubber.

To survive in the surplus society we need more innovation. Innovation means creating what is not. Innovation is about creating things the world hasn't seen before. Innovation is about asking 'What if?' then asking it again, and again, and again. This partly explains why entrepreneurs are sometimes difficult to deal with. While most journalists, academics, managers and civil servants deal with what is, these people do exactly the opposite.

Innovation requires experimentation. Experiments are risky. We can succeed or fail. So, an innovative environment must have an exceptionally high tolerance for mistakes. And so must leaders of innovative organisations. In a sense failure lies at the very heart of a market economy. In experimentation, we should forgive while never forgetting what we have learned. According to Deepak Sethi, CEO of Organic Leadership, the organisation of tomorrow will actually *demand* mistakes and failures. We have got to fail faster to learn quicker and succeed sooner. 'Failure is just part of the culture of innovation. Accept it and become stronger,' advised Albert Yu when he was a senior vice-president at Intel. In Silicon Valley, failure is not a black dot – it is a badge of achievement.

The trouble is that traditional organisations are not the most forgiving of environments. In many firms, failure carries the corporate equivalent of the death penalty. If you make a mistake, corporate Siberia beckons. This sends a signal to the corporate system that failure is punished. This not only stops people from failing – it stops them from trying. It leads to the building of systems that act against innovation rather than ones that nurture innovation.

True innovators are prepared to fail in pursuit of unknown territories – *terra incognita* instead of *terra firma*. The pursuit of difference and creativity is ridden with astonishing twists and turns. During the last century, the success of Mahathma Ghandi's India, Henry Ford's Model T, Man Ray's photographs, Ruben Rausing's TetraPak, the Beatles' Sgt Pepper's album, the Fosbery flop in athletics, Akito Morita's Sony Walkman, Muhammad Yunus' microbanking and Apple's iPod can all be attributed to their unusual ability to combine new technology, institutions and values in unexpected ways. They took risks. They surprised people and, probably, themselves.

Some risk their lives in pursuit of creating something new and different. The great value innovator Jesus took risks and was crucified. In our times, Nelson Mandela took risks and almost died for it. Alfred Nobel took risks and passed away in solitude. Van Gogh took risks, was ridiculed and committed suicide. For every Bill Gates and Michael Dell, or any other well-known, risk-prone explorer, there are thousands and thousands of others who tried and failed. They lost their families, friends, fortunes, dignity and sometimes, ultimately, their lives. Our thoughts should go out to all those forgotten heroes who tried and failed. We should hail them, because the innermost mechanism of human progress is called failure. If it were not for all the fools trying to do the impossible – over and over again – we would still be living in caves.

Traditionalists should remember that the only way not to fail is not to try. And try we must. No failures; no development. Philosopher Ludwig Wittgenstein even argued that, 'If people never did silly things, nothing intelligent would ever happen.'

Respect is therefore due to all who take risks. Companies must become breeding grounds of risk takers. To do so requires a huge shift. In military action, great importance is attached to taking care of the wounded and seeking out those missing in action. How else could you keep morale up? In the French Foreign Legion you receive a medal if you are wounded. Taking reasonable, calculated risks (a classical contradiction in terms) is what you are there for. If the wounded were quickly shunted away and ignored as failures, morale would plummet. Yet, that is what happens in many organisations.

But not in all. Think, for example, of these corporate disasters.

First, one of the most talked of corporate mishaps of the modern era: the 1985 decision by Coca-Cola to replace its traditional recipe cola with New Coke. In detailed research it had discovered that most consumers preferred the new recipe. It was, they said, smoother, sweeter and preferable to the old version. This conveniently overlooked the fact that the old version was selling in many millions every day of the week. It also overlooked the fact that people who buy a Coke buy something more and something else than the mere atoms. To call this the marketing own-goal of the century would

Alfred Nobel

NAT
MDCCC
XXXIII
OB
MDCCC
XCVI

ALFR·
NOBEL

be to understate the effect only slightly. Coke was faced with a barrage of criticism. On the other hand, its archrival Pepsi could barely contain its glee – indeed, it quickly produced advertising which was extremely gleeful, rubbing in the fact that 'the real thing' remained unchanged.

Realising that its move had been disastrous, Coke backtracked and, after 90 days, reintroduced the original Coke. It has not been tinkered with since. So, did heads roll? Did the Coca-Cola chief, Roberto Goizueta, immediately head to the door marked exit? No. In fact, not a single person from the management team left because of the New Coke disaster.

Second, there was GE's experience with Kidder Peabody. Big bucks were lost and the deal remains one of the few blemishes on GE chief Jack Welch's record. In 1986 GE bought 80 per cent of Kidder Peabody for $600 million. The Kidder debacle cost GE $1.2 billion. 'I've rewarded failures by giving out awards to people when they've failed, because they took a swing,' says Welch. 'Keep taking swings. I teach a course at Crotonville (the GE training centre) for six hours – four to six hours – on leadership. I always say, if the chairman can buy Kidder Peabody and mess it up, you can do about anything. It was on the front page of *The Wall Street Journal* 19 times. Now, if the chairman can do that and still survive, you ought to be able to take swings everywhere. You can hardly do worse.'

Similarly, the CEO of one major US corporation handed out awards for Best Failures during his senior executive forum. Jaws dropped at the very thought. This represented a major cultural shift in that only a year before failures – especially big or public ones – were to be hidden not celebrated.

It is a fact that the most intensive learning experiences tend to occur when we fail rather than when we succeed. 'Most of the things I have learnt were not learned formally but through accidents and failure. I learned from small catastrophes,' admits Charles Handy. He is not alone. Most of us learn in such a haphazard and occasionally unhappy way. If there were awards for Best Failures we would have a large number to choose from.

Failure happens. Give people trust and it will happen more productively. We are not saying that leaders should promote risk-taking per se. Rather, it is a question of making it less risky to take risk. Work at Decision Research, a company based in Eugene, Oregon studying risk management strategies, suggests that people are more likely to accept risks that they perceive as voluntarily undertaken, controllable, understandable and equally distributed. And, conversely, people are less willing to take risks that they don't understand and which are unfairly distributed.

Give people freedom and they will pursue their own creative by-ways. Give people time and you don't know what creative results will emerge – slack is a prerequisite for innovation. 3M does just that with its 15 per cent policy – researchers can spend up to 15 per cent of their time on their own projects. The 15 per cent policy is called, among other things, 'the bootleg policy'. It may also be called a competitive advantage because it has helped foster and nurture so many good ideas – most notably the Post-It.

The 15 per cent policy encourages researchers to roam further afield. Fujio Mitarai, CEO and the president of Canon, has said, 'We should do something when people say it is crazy. If people say something is good, it means that someone else is already doing it.' Along similar lines, Nobel Laureate Arno Penzias of Bell Labs says, 'The definition of a lousy product is one that has no enemies within the company.'

The aim should be the creation of a bubbling ferment of ideas. 'The object is to spur as many ideas as possible because perhaps 1 in 1000 will turn out to fit,' explains Post-It note developer Art Fry. 'An idea might be a perfectly good idea for another company, but not for yours. Putting together a new product is like putting together a jigsaw puzzle such as raw material suppliers, distributors, government regulations and the amount of capital you have to spend. If one part doesn't fit, the whole project can fail. Your work might have been brilliant but somebody else dropping the ball can lead to failure.'

From the desk of the CDO

And, in an age of abundance, no organisation or leader can rest on their laurels. Innovation means competing with yourself. The key message sent to product development teams in Silicon Valley is 'Obsolete your own products'. Most companies do not need more CEOs – they need a couple of CDOs, chief destruction officers, people who destroy the old cash cows by creating new ones. If you are not willing to commit to this act of creative destruction, rest assured that your competitors are. We better start eating our lunches before someone else does. Or, as Adam Smith put it more than 200 years ago, 'It takes a lot of ruin to make the wealth of a great nation.' The same reasoning applies to all companies, regardless of age, size, industry and geographical origin.

Education – Develop Me

In a brain-based world, we have to change our definition of education and training. We used to believe in taking a huge overdose of education until the age of 25. The theory was that this massive infusion of education would keep us high and flying for the next 40 years or so, and after that no one would need us anymore.

This approach to learning means that for the majority of people's lives learning wasn't even on their agenda. It was generic and broad ranging rather than personalised and targeted. It overlooked the fact that education is not about filling people's heads with facts. It is emotion and soul. It is personal.

In a world where competitive advantages can be found softwhere, education needs to be continuous and lifelong. Education is a competitive weapon – for individuals as well as firms. The workplace has to become a campus. If you want to attract and retain the best people, you will have to train them. Or, as James Sims, CEO at Cambridge Technology Partners, puts it, 'Most people will have seven jobs before their career is over. What they look for in an employer is a continuous investment in their career.' Sims' company spends 7 per cent of sales on training – 18 times more than the average US firm.

The reality is that employee education isn't growing 100 per cent faster than academia, but 100 times or 10,000 per cent faster.

Companies are setting up their own 'universities' to train tomorrow's executives. There are now thousands of corporate universities worldwide covering virtually every industry. On the surface these are not institutions which the denizens of Harvard are likely to lose sleep over. McDonald's Hamburger University in Oak Brook, Illinois lacks academic *gravitas*. But, in over 45 years it has produced more than 80,000 graduates and has 30 resident professors delivering programmes in 22 languages.

Corporate universities are not solely a US phenomenon. In April 1998, British Aerospace unveiled plans to create its own virtual university, called the British Aerospace Virtual University, in partnership with outside academic institutions. In the next decade, it pledged to invest more than £1.5 billion in building the company's 'knowledge base'. It provided 19,600 online courses and 323,854 online training hours in 2004.

Sceptics may shake their heads at the very idea of Hamburger University or Disney University, but the rate at which corporate universities are opening suggests that major corporations take them very seriously. Perhaps the best known corporate university is that run by Motorola. The Motorola University, 'an instrument of renewal' according to the company, supplies 550,000 student days a year and costs $170 million. Every single Motorola employee – and there are 139,000 – is expected to receive at least 40 hours of training per year. The company has also developed its own international MBA programme. Motorola calculates that every dollar invested in training reaps $33.

Changing educational needs will produce changing educational institutions. 'Universities won't survive. The future is outside the traditional campus, outside the traditional classroom. Distance learning is coming on fast,' predicted no less a sage than Peter Drucker. While as long ago as 1994, futurists Stan Davis and Jim Botkin foresaw, 'the school house of the future may be neither school nor house'.

Technology is revolutionising education. Traditional institutions, such as universities and business schools, have done nothing while upstarts have stolen a march. Soon even bigger corporations will become involved in education. When media group Pearson bought Simon & Schuster's education, reference and business and professional publishing activities for $3.6 billion in 1998, education was the top of its agenda. 'Education is one of the great growth industries of our time,' pronounced Pearson chief executive, Marjorie Scardino who decided to focus Pearson as a media and educational company, selling such unrelated properties as Madame Tussaud's Waxworks and purchasing various educational and publishing properties. Companies such as Microsoft, Disney and News Corporation are also eyeing the opportunities. Michael Milken, the junk bond king, after a spell behind bars, has become an important investor and benefactor in the fields of education, medicine and technology. He has seen the future.

Amid this welcome and overdue maelstrom of activity, the nature of education has fundamentally changed and will continue to do so. Learning is now increasingly regarded as lifelong – though exactly what this means or entails is often a little vague – and it is also regarded as personal.

Since a lot of knowledge is tacit and difficult to communicate, learning can by no means be restricted to the 'classroom'. We must also learn on the job. We have to turn the workplace into a gas station for our brains, not only a racetrack. Development and education is as much about improving the processes in which we work and getting to know the people around us as it is about reading yet another book or listening to another lecture. Development is about mentoring, training disciples and coaching. It is the job of leaders to create new leaders. Leadership is about contaminating and being contaminated with knowledge. The distinction between learning, working and living is gone – it is one and the same thing.

Personalisation – See Me

Today, most companies excel in responding to complaints, requests and all other whimsies from core customers. They do so in a few hours or sometimes even a few minutes. Yet, suggestions and questions from core competents – the stars, who don't happen to be top managers – are often not even taken seriously. Remember what Larry Bossidy at Allied Signal said, 'At the end of the day we bet on people, not strategies.'

At your firm, are the employees treated as investors? Because this is what they are – intellectual investors. Every day they bring their heads and hearts to work. And if they don't, you will soon be extinct. We must treat our people like

A prescient remark perhaps. Prince reverted to his original stage name in 2000, left Warner, and released material as an independent and over the Internet. His last two albums have been one-album-only deals with Columbia and Universal, with the labels distributing but Prince still picking up a good royalty. So the balance of power may have shifted to the artist in this instance.

volunteers. Maybe we should ask the Red Cross or the Salvation Army to share their secrets with us?

And any lack of attention is more problematic for the firm than for the individual members. The organisation is disposable – the stars will keep on shining. If, for one reason or another, CNN goes down the drain, it's not detrimental to Larry King. If Alessi goes bankrupt, designer Philippe Starck may shed a tear, but soon he's back on track. If Harvard Business School has to close down the store, Professor Rosabeth Moss Kanter just moves on. If Warner is teetering on the abyss, the artist formerly known as Prince is unlikely to have sleepless nights. In an age where capital is abundant, the bargaining power of Larry, Philippe, Rosabeth and the Symbol is increasing by the hour, by the minute, by the second. The only thing that now makes capital dance is talent. And it's not every second dance – capital is engaged in a non-stop St Vitus dance.

People differ

Human beings are not bulk goods. They come in different shapes and forms. Each and every individual is different. Every now and then this is brought to our attention. But change takes time. It took the car industry close to 100 years to realise that women are not small men. In the Funky Fragmented Village, we can look forward to further differentiation of individuals and their needs. One-to-one everything.

You either manage this differentiation or you watch as your most precious assets walk out of the door. If you educate people and then treat them as morons or just a human resource, the best ones will leave. Education without personalisation treats training as a cost rather than an investment.

To attract and retain good men and women we have to treat them as individuals. The word *individual* originates from Latin and literally means indivisible. We are moving towards one-to-one leadership. The consequence is that each

Leaders must ask themselves if they are really prepared to surrender their own egos to others.

and every little system needs to be personalised. People can be treated and approached, evaluated and rewarded, motivated and inspired in a number of different ways. At the companies voted most popular to work for in the US, the employees are offered things such as on-the-job massages, dry cleaning or a personal concierge. We are all unique individuals. Dress code at Sun Microsystems = You must.

The highly successful software company SAS Institute in North Carolina has no limits on sick-days. You can even stay home to take care of sick family members. The firm is responsible for the largest daycare operations in the state. People work a 35-hour week and there are baby seats in the lunchroom. Pampering? Sure, but if you can't pamper your own people you are hardly likely to pamper your customers and go that extra mile to enhance their experience.

People differ and what motivates them differs

People are motivated by different things, in different ways and at different times. What motivates you does not motivate me, and what motivates your colleagues does not necessarily motivate us. To prevent total chaos, funky organisations must appeal to a tribe of people with some commonality in attitude. Think about the cases of SouthWest Airlines and McKinsey. The lowest common denominator allows us to differ in any other dimension. So, some people may say, 'But I don't work with my friends – those who share my vibes.' Well, do you want to change employer or friends?

And these values are not inevitably concerned with money. Not for all people. 'Too many organisations seem to believe that the only motivation to work is an economic one. Treating knowledge assets like Skinnerian rats is hardly the way to get the best out of people' says strategy guru Gary Hamel. Instead of being provided with detailed job descriptions, employees should provide managers with motivation descriptions.

In the well-known Maslowian hierarchy of needs, we all start at the bottom with satisfying our hunger and then slowly move towards self-realisation. Today, things are turned upside down.

Many people go for self-realisation first – then the rest. They are prepared to starve for a few weeks to be able to buy a piece of art, a BMW mountain-bike (they do exist and are predictably expensive), a portable PlayStation, a cool outfit from We The Superlative Conspiracy, or to travel to the Himalayas.

Increasingly, motivation is based on values as well as cash. Historically, loyalty was basically bought. The employer offered gradual progression up the hierarchy, a decent salary and job security. In return, the employee offered unwavering loyalty and a hard day's work. Now, values determine loyalty. 'Every organisation needs values, but a lean organisation needs them even more,' Jack Welch says. 'When you strip away the support systems of staffs and layers, people have to change their habits and expectations, or else the stress will just overwhelm them.' The challenge for organisations is that values are more complex than mere money. Values cannot be simplistically condensed into a mission statement or neatly printed onto an embossed card. And values cannot be invented. Either we have them or we don't.

By having and communicating a clear set of values, the organisation becomes self-selecting – it primarily attracts people who share that attitude. Being fuzzy means that anyone or no one will knock on the door. Remember that it is a buyer's market. The competents are in charge. For stars there is a choice. They work for companies that are in accord with their own value systems. If they don't want to work for a polluter, they will not. After all, people want to hold their heads up when they are with their peers. They don't want an embarrassed silence when they announce whom they work for. 'These days we value a great mission and a great working lifestyle as much as a bigger desk and the prospect of promotion,' says publisher Richard Stagg. 'Who gets out of bed in the morning for a distant corporate objective? If a company gives real meaning to people's work and the freedom and resources to pursue their ideas then it's a good place to be.'

*If people differ and their motivations differ, rewards
must differ*

We are used to differentiated contracts in every other market
but not in the labour market. While standard contracts are
acceptable in a mass production context they are hardly
applicable to a building full of highly charged brains with widely
different reasons for being there. Celebrities want customised
working hours, rewards, perks, office furniture and so on. And
not only global executives qualify as celebrities. We are talking
about janitors, programmers, teachers and sales reps – anyone
who is really good at what he or she is doing.

We live in a world in which working contracts are
increasingly individual and individualistic. People will express
themselves through their contracts. You are your contract, and
your contract is you. The
Brazilian soccer player,
Edmundo, had written into
his contract with Italian
team Fiorentina that he
had a two-week vacation
during the Rio Carnival.
Excessive? Perhaps it is,
but what if it maximises

**Currently with Brazilian team
Palmeiras. The carnival is in
February and the football
season finishes in
December, so he shouldn't
need a similar contract.**

his performance during the rest of the football season?

The emerging system will have to share the profits with its
talents. We are moving towards an outright star system. We
trade in talents and, as a result, can expect much more
sophisticated and diverse contracts between single individuals
and business firms. Business-to-business contracts are in
most cases tailor made. Transaction-specific. Brains and their
owners are not homogenous. They are unique, so the
transaction-specificity increases. This must be reflected in
employment contracts.

People differ and the only way you will find out how much they differ is by listening to them

Blind loyalty is undoubtedly dead. Corporate man is now (in certain industries and countries) even more likely to be corporate woman. 'Passive obedience was once mistaken for loyalty. The entire notion of loyalty was wrapped up with control. Now, people are not loyal in a slavish sense,' a business psychologist told us. 'This is based on the realisation that you can question the system without being disloyal.'

Today's employees are more questioning and demanding. Remember, they have the freedom to know, go, do and be. They are confident enough to air their concerns, grievances and aspirations. If they were customers, we would call them sophisticated. It is perhaps significant that we tend not to. Maybe we should? Perhaps we must.

To handle variety, funky leaders expose themselves to more diverse experiences. Nathan Myhrvold also worked as an assistant chef at a French restaurant in Seattle. Ole Bek of the Danish consumer electronics company Bang & Olufsen claims that he 'learns much more window-shopping at Louis Vuitton in Paris than by looking at consumer electronics outlets'. To get some fresh input visit art galleries, go to parties, listen to opera, hang out with alcoholics or druggies, read stuff that you are not really interested in – do anything that you have never done before. Try it out – surf the web, go skydiving, visit a museum.

COMING OUT

The great socialist project – the dream of handing over power to the people – is being realised in front of our eyes. It is being realised, not by the disciples of Communism, but by the preachers of free enterprise and market capitalism. An organisation such as Manpower, the world's largest temp and talent agency, with some 600,000 individual partners, is essentially an international trade union like any other temp agency, an employment bureau for selected global specialists.

The large multinationals roaming the globe, dominating the world economy, are much the same thing – at least for those with skills scarce enough to qualify as employable.

We have to take control over our lives

In such a world, we have to be absolutely clear about who we are, where we want to go, and who we want to do business with, hang around with, have a relationship with and so on. If we are all condemned to freedom, we have to take control over our own lives. We can't rely on the church, the mosque or the temple, the state or any other stable institution to supply our lives with meaning any more. For us as individuals, all this implies: More freedom = more opportunities = more power = more responsibility.

None of this has anything to do with politics. We are simply talking about the logical consequences of the forces of funk. It is built on insight, and insights cannot be legislated against.

Funky freedom is apolitical, until we pose the more critical question of if and how these forces could be put to good use in the realisation of a good life. To answer this requires a new

Technology is driven by human curiosity. Try to stop that!

vision of the good life – a vision that actually means something to people living in the twenty-first, rather than twentieth century. Meanwhile, what is, is.

In a do-it-yourself Welfare State it is all up to the individual. For better or worse, there is no one else to rely on or to blame. It is time to become head of our own head, and determinator of our own destiny. It is time to come out. The slogan of our times is UBU – you be you. The masquerade is over. Denial equals death. Successful people are successful because they are what they do and they do what they are. This begins by ridding ourselves of the roles imposed on us. We must strip down to our personality. We must ask who am I? If you dare to undress to your barest bones, you are not a mother or a father, not a manager or a subordinate, not Coloured or Caucasian, not European, Asian or American. What is left? What do you really want to do with your life? The power is in your hands.

In order to thrive in this global, hyper-competitive environment, we need to develop a personal strategy. We need a survival kit and we need to put it together now. Good times are not around the corner unless you take a look down a lot of blind alleys.

If you aren't enjoying what you are doing – quit doing it. And quit immediately. Just listen to master investor Warren Buffett when he says, 'I always worry about people who say "I'm going to do this for ten years; I really don't like it very much. And then I'll do this..." That's a little bit like saving sex for your old age.' Shopping and fucking wait for no one.

Three key things will characterise the successful funkster. These three simple traits are valid no matter your age, gender, race, geographical origin, educational background or occupation.

Be *Unique*

Regardless of what you do, to be successful you need to be unique, at least for a moment in time. We must all strive to establish monopolies. At the same time, we have to be true to what and who we are. Nothing else will do. In a totally transparent society, we can no longer pretend to work or try to be someone else. Historically, people who were different had a hard time. Now, deviance from the norm is the recipe for survival.

It's 1976. You have $5,000 in your bank account and are soon to be 25. What are you going to do?

A throw one hell of a party,

B buy a used car,

C start a venture capital company investing in IT entrepreneurs?

Ask Ann Winblad of Hummer Winblad, one of the most successful venture capital firms in the world.

It's 1977. You have $2,000 in your bank account and are soon to be 33. What are you going to do:

A throw one hell of a party,

B buy a used car,

C start a database company?

Ask Larry Ellison, founder and CEO of Oracle.

It's 1984. You have $1,000 in your bank account and are soon to be 19. What are you going to do:

A throw one hell of a party,

B buy a used car,

C start selling PCs from your dorm room?

Ask Michael Dell.

It's 2007. What are you going to do?

The new champions will be the IWCs – idea-generators without capital – and the losers will be known as CWIs – capitalists without ideas. Talent makes capital dance.

There are basically two ways to go. First, there is the hyper-specialist such as the late Red Adair, the guy who travelled around the world to put out fires in oilfields. You could become an expert on a specific type of eczema, pastry, sport, musical instrument, or whatever. Focus, focus, focus and then go global.

Second, you strive to be a successful hyphenist by combining opposites. Performance-technologists, visual-ergonomists, psycho-linguists and compu-ecologists already walk the earth.

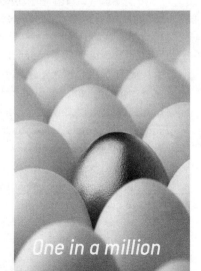

One in a million

Incorporate

Today, people can and do go public. Look at David Bowie. He has issued bonds on 25 albums with 300 songs – making some $60 million in doing so. Ziggy Stardust, the thin white Duke, is not alone. Doctors do it. Journalists do it. Professors do it. Programmers are doing it. We can all do it.

During the past 20 years the number of self-employed people in the US has increased by 100 per cent. In Europe, we see a similar trend. People are leaving their companies because their talents are being ignored, misused or not rewarded enough in terms of cash and/or recognition. They depart to set up their own companies – Moi S.A, Me plc, Jag AB, Ich Gmbh, Jeg AS, Me Inc. – business units of one. They will often continue doing the same thing, but charge twice as much, re-selling their knowledge to former employers and others.

The number of businesses with no paid employees in the US grew from 17.6 million in 2002 to more than 18.6 million in 2003, a growth rate of 5.7 per cent. This represents the biggest rate of increase in self-employment since the Census Bureau began releasing such statistics in 1997.

Andy Warhol was right. However, he may have been exaggerating by around fourteen and a half minutes. If we look upon our work-life as a series of gigs or projects rather than a career, constant re-creation of yourself is a necessity. And you are never better than your last gig. We must look upon ourselves as a company with our own intellectual balance sheet and brand name. We need to invest in ourselves and market ourselves. Rather than employment security, funky people go for employability – constantly updating their skills so that they are desirable to potential employers all the time and at any time.

But skills are only part of the story. Funky people also work hard to create attention and attraction. They must, because they are all players in the great global attraction game. There

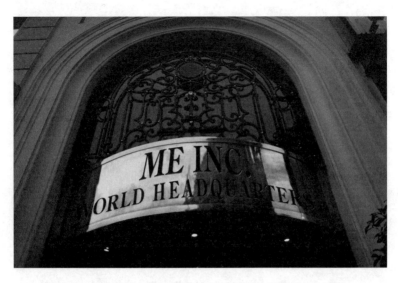

is a surplus of most of the skills that people embody. Incorporation is not only a question of education – investing in personal R&D. More education in itself will not solve the problem. Just look at all the MBAs or engineers. However nice the credentials, they are just faces in a very large crowd of people with similar basic training. Attraction and attention are not only a case of content, but also of form. We must brand, package and market ourselves so that we are desirable. Under what slogan will you be sold?

Get Connected

Nothing the slightest amazing has ever been done in isolation. Get ready for mingle mania. In a surplus society you are only as strong as the people you know. You may well be the smartest person in the world but if no one is aware of you it doesn't make any difference. Individual competitiveness = What you know × Who you know. Overnight, each and every one of us could set up a multinational company in our garage. Using the Internet, we can reach a potential market of billions of people.

Focus, focus, focus, and then focus again means that we all need to find partners. We need to find partners that help us with each and every little activity and process where we are not world-class. A lot of people are used to outsourcing parts of their private lives – cleaning, daycare, etc. Now it is time to start farming out part of our working life. You need to find partners that enable you to be you. These guys are your world-class back-office, factory, marketing department, whatever. They leverage your capabilities. They allow you to come out and reach out.

Partnership power means that we will witness the emergence of dynamic clusters of expertise and knowledge. This will be fuelled by greater global mobility. In the past people largely stayed where they were born or educated. Some countries encouraged this by not allowing you to move your assets elsewhere. Now, money and talent flow more freely.

The result will be that people will follow the leaders in their field. If countries can't close the door, they will have to provide magnets so that resources and people gravitate towards them. It is like having a party and planning who will be there. Play hip-hop and the hip-hop crowd will find their way there.

We will see the redistribution of people along tribal lines. The map of Europe and of the world will be redrawn. The United Clusters of Europe may be around the corner. Scandinavia could be home to the music cluster or become a female nirvana. Already, in India there is the Goan hippie cluster. The UK has the financial cluster in London. In the US, Vermont could be the media cluster. There is the Formula One racing cluster in Oxfordshire, UK, the automotive cluster in Germany, the tile cluster in northern Italy. The cluster map of the world will constantly change as people move around, forming new partnerships and permutations. The important stuff – tacit knowledge – still demands a level of human interaction. You have to be breathing the same air.

DREAMANAGEMENT

We are all leaders now. We may not all be leading the Googles and IBMs of the world, but we are all leaders. We have to be. We need to lead our own lives. Leadership is no longer something you do occasionally; it goes on every day all the time. Everything you do is leadership because you are always trying to get people to buy into what you are doing. And you are always trying to figure out who you really are. True leaders do not practise leadership – they live leadership. They are what they do.

The development of leaders has gone through three phases. The first generation of business leaders were often lawyers. As the limited company was a new phenomenon, the critical knowledge required to run corporations was related to judicial matters – the legal flow. Experts were needed. Time went by. Knowledge spread. Rather than legal matters, technology became the great bean-feast. As a result, the second generation of leaders generally had an engineering background. This made sense at a time when competitive advantages came from technological innovations. Leaders managed the product flow. As time passed, new dimensions were added. Organisational and money matters became the focal point. The third generation of leaders were MBAs. They managed the financial and administrative flows.

Now everything is a question of intelligence, talent and intangibles – knowledge flows. A great deal of critical knowledge resides in individuals. This implies that leadership is a matter of attracting and retaining great people – managing the attention flow. In turn, this means providing meaning and identity for a certain tribe. And, as leaders, we must constantly re-create this forcefield of attraction and attention. It is kick-off time every day, every hour, every second. In a world where power belongs to the people, all leaders must become *humanagers*.

While a lot of people continue to believe in old-style leadership and management, they are doomed to fail. Few people admit to being lousy lovers; even fewer bosses admit to being lousy leaders. Soon, many will have to.

In organisation after organisation leadership is being passed on to a new type of leader. In the funky village the fuckers and shoppers have already taken over. Good or bad? It is a fact of life. The front page of *Fortune* trumpeted 'Addicted to Sex' – corporate America's dirty little secret. The cover story was a 10-page journey into the shadowlands of egomania. Freud was right: sex is all. And not only for youngsters. Just remember William Jefferson Clinton.

Little wonder then that the search for meaning is on. Look, for example, at the development of the self-help genre. Books on personal awareness abound as people try to understand themselves and their environment. The searching is an inevitable side effect of the new world order. Our previous vision of the good life – a house, washing machine, steady job, etc. – has been undermined. Its replacement is not easily found. As a result, people shop to build an identity. Their purchases express which tribe they would like to belong to. Power exists – as it always has – in providing people with dreams. Dreams that touch people, excite and arouse them. Once it was Marx, Kennedy and Martin Luther King who brought us dreams. Now, it is Michael Dell, Steve Jobs, Anthony Robbins and Stephen Covey. In a world of diversity, a world of tribes, their dreams mean everything and nothing. The question must be how you can provide relevant and potent dreams for the tribes of the world.

'*All business is show business*' Jan Carlzon

6 FEELING

Are you ready to do business in a world with close to friction-free markets for anything from components to capital, from whale oil to engine lubricants, from perfume to alcohol? Are you ready to design, staff and manage organisations that permit us to practise total innovation? Are you ready to take care of your own life, career and capabilities?

Let's face it, in a knockdown welfare state we have to build our own support systems, map out our own futures. And we have to deal with people who are motivated by anything but celibacy and savings.

That is a lot of balls to juggle in the air at the same time. Making it work is the ultimate circus act. Perhaps it is all possible. Perhaps we can catch them all as they fall towards the ground simultaneously. Perhaps we can't. The trouble is that, even if we do, it is not enough. Juggling all those balls and catching them is not enough to guarantee future success. The truth is hard to take. Juggling the balls and being able to catch them is unfortunately only a necessary, but not sufficient, condition for securing survival in a surplus society.

New balls are being continually tossed in the air. They may even be invisible. The age of abundance is slowly turning into the age of affection. Surplus must be handled not by doing more of the same but by introducing elements of sentiment and sensation. In an excess economy, the sources underlying competitiveness have shifted towards things that we cannot touch. Ethereal commerce. Both potential customers and prospective employees will cry out for products, services, strategies, leaders and organisations that touch them.

E(motional) commerce. We all want to be touched. We crave attention. The rest is triviality.

Alberto Alessi did it with toilet brushes in Milan. Richard Branson is doing it with the pensions business in the UK. Steve Jobs is doing it with iPods in San Francisco. Nokia is doing it with mobile phones in Helsinki. They have all realised that we must now exploit the last taboo. The sensational society demands that we base our competitiveness on feelings and fantasy.

WET DREAMS ARE MADE OF THIS

Think Progressive. Think Dell. Think IKEA. Think Chevrolet Suburban. Think Starbucks. Lucrative opportunities exist everywhere. Business is not rocket science. It basically boils down to making money. Now, this may not be the reason why successful companies are founded in the first place. Remember Disney and Ford setting out to respectively make people happy and democratise the automobile. For them money was just a positive result of a much greater purpose. Or, as the famous Austrian psychiatrist Victor Frankl so eloquently once put it: 'For success, like happiness cannot be pursued, it must ensue... as the unintended side effect of one's personal dedication to a course greater than oneself.'

Greater purposes or not, all business firms need to show a profit. And in a market economy, there is but one way to make money. This explains why all managers around the world, regardless of age, gender, geographical origin and educational background, share the same wet dream. Despite all the talk about the superiority of the capitalist system and the necessity of cut-throat competition, every night, all over the globe, each and every one of these managers dreams about finding the Holy Grail of business – a temporary monopoly. And so do musicians, artists, doctors, lawyers and so on. It is the universal wet dream.

In fact, creating temporary monopolies is exactly what managers are paid to do, and often quite handsomely. Only when we are in a monopoly position can we charge prices that allow above average profits. It may be a geographical monopoly or a product/service monopoly. If you were in the happy position of owning one, you probably wouldn't care what category it fell under.

Unfortunately, the word monopoly has had a bad press. Announcing that your core strategy is to create temporary monopolies would not be a sound business move. Customers would flee and the authorities would move in. To save you from such indignities, we suggest you refer to niches rather than monopolies – though the meaning is exactly the same.

By focusing on a specific tribe – a geographical market or certain customers – we hope to avoid competition and price wars. We want to be perceived as the only natural 'choice' for our target customers, by leaving them with no choice. Beauty really is in the eye of the

Apple's ad slogan for the iMac was the brilliant: 'Chic. Not geek'.

beholder. To be a successful niche competitor you need to be different. Funky firms follow the advice of the computer company Apple: they Think Different – then they rethink it again. We all want products or services that are unique in some respect – offerings that capture the attention of a specific tribe.

Basically, there are only two ways in which you can be different – either you are perceived as cheaper or you are perceived as better. But uniqueness is not only a question of the customer offering as such. There is nothing particularly original about the *products* of a company such as Dell. Uniqueness can come from anything – an idea, the business logic, the packaging, the culture or the people.

The same is true in nature: survival is based on being fit or sexy – adapt, attract or become extinct.

Being different is the key. That's why firms are so dependent on people who can come up with unique ideas. The trouble is that uniqueness and difference are often the preserve of people who, judged against the average corporate citizen, are a little strange, not to say weird. These are the true entrepreneurs, people prepared to challenge the status quo, to look at the world with totally open eyes, break the rules, ignore regulations and question the norms. They are prepared to take risks, personal risks. The question must be whether we are willing to take risks. Would you and your organisation take risks in the quest for temporary monopolies?

Of course, there is only one answer because there is no longer any choice. Normality is the route to nowhere. If we are only willing to behave like all the others, we will see the same things, hear the same things, hire similar people, come up with similar ideas and develop identical products or services. We will drown in the sea of normality. And Normal Inc. is bankrupt.

Abnormality creates monopolies – our 15 minutes of capitalist fame. And, if weirdness is the only way to wealth, think again about the weird-factor at your organisation. Is it really high enough? Opportunities are just waiting to be discovered, but we have to look at unexplored places – places where our competitors have not already been 343 times. Otherwise we are doomed to see what all the others have already seen. Monopolists make money.

From Location to Organisation

If you don't believe us, consider the evolution of competitiveness. In the beginning, competitive advantage was primarily derived from location. Access to various raw materials provided the firm-specific advantages necessary to create and exploit temporary monopolies. The successful company of the nineteenth century profited from access to oil, forests, mines, etc. and made families, such as the Rockefellers and the Gettys, incredibly rich. It was a question of finding and exploiting the Klondikes of the world.

But the capitalist economy is ruthless. Soon, free markets for raw materials made it increasingly difficult to use location as the single source of competitive advantage. As this happened, innovation and technology, combined with access to capital, became the new differentiators. The key to competitiveness was creating more value out of the same input. As a result, at the turn of the twentieth century, the business community was dominated by a few capitalists and a number of innovatory entrepreneurs – people like the Wallenbergs, Thomas Alva Edison, JP Morgan, Alfred Nobel, the Rothschilds and Otto Diesel. Competitive edge was based on ingenuity.

Once again the market struck back. Products were imitated and patents were sold or acquired. When these innovations were turned into everyone's property, competitive advantage could no longer be based on a now defunct technological monopoly.

We then entered the organisational age. Pioneers such as Alfred P. Sloan and Henry DuPont in the US designed the multidivisional firm – splitting up the company into smaller, product-focused units. The new organisation allowed a continuous upgrading of previous technological advantages. This organisational innovation became the dominant model for most large and complex US firms, allowing them to conquer the world. It made sense given that all firms exploited similar technologies. The ones with superior organisational solutions succeeded. Later, European firms adopted the model and the international competitive playing field was forced to the horizontal.

Progressively, throughout the latter half of the twentieth century, a plethora of organisational innovations have given rise to minor and major temporary monopolies. Just in time (JIT), business process re-engineering (BPR), management by objectives (MBO), total quality management (TQM), management by walking around (MBWA), kanban, benchmarking, matrix management, outsourcing, downsizing, strategic alliances and lean production – the list could go on ad infinitum – have all created a glimmer of competitive advantage for those who were first to fully capitalise on them. For most, as always, the glimmer was a distant and fleeting glimpse.

*Access to
forests made
families
incredibly
rich*

The organisation has moved on. Gone (theoretically, at
least) is the bureaucratic firm described by Max Weber almost
a century ago. Right now, if you belong to the organisational
in-crowd, your firm is supposed to look like a blueberry
pancake, a fishnet, a shamrock, gazelles, or even boiling
spaghetti. Most modern firms still base their competitiveness
on developing an organisational solution that enables them to
uphold a fruitful balance between exploiting givens and
creating novelty.

In a world of surpluses, novelty is usually in short supply.
Companies, managers and human beings have a lemming-like
capacity to follow each other. Sameness is infectious; karaoke
behaviour. In search of organisational inspiration, companies
turn to global consulting companies. They see a competitor
that has re-engineered, so they hire a consultant to design a
re-engineering programme for them. The dominoes fall. Soon
most companies in an industry have been re-engineered. The
consulting firms are better off. But there is little in the way of

competitive advantage to be extracted from doing something everyone else has already done. McKinsey & Company, Boston Consulting Group and Cap Gemini, to name but a few, all contribute to the current homogenisation of organisational solutions around the world.

Not only that. Think about all the MBA students and those people who get a masters degree in science. Every year they invade companies around the world. As competent as they may be, they belong to a group of globally standardised individuals. Whether you go to a business or engineering school in Moscow or Manila, Seattle or San Sebastian does not really matter. You are exposed to the same models, books and formulas. These students are then let loose, equipped with identical recipes for how to succeed.

Similarly, the introduction of information technology has given certain companies initial advantages. But, as virtually all firms become wired, IT will act as a homogenising force, making company organisations ever more similar. Technology tends to have that effect. Just think of what has happened to cars after the introduction of wind

It's a bit like having access to a toilet at the office – necessary but not sufficient for the creation of sustainable competitive advantages.

tunnels and CAD/CAM. When we were young and our parents took us out for a drive, we competed with our younger brothers trying to guess the brands of the cars that passed us. Today, who can tell the difference?

Karaoke everything! Sameness is a fact. Ericsson must have world-class, top-of-the-line technology. It must pioneer new organisational solutions. The firm needs the best IT solutions that money can buy. Ericsson must attract, recruit and retain the top people on the job market. It must work with the best suppliers in the world, not the closest. All this is necessary. There is no choice. But it is not sufficient because Nokia is also doing it. LG is doing it. Motorola is doing it. Sony is doing it. Samsung is doing it. They are all doing it.

The consequence is that competitiveness can no longer be solely based on location, technological innovation, or organisation. Any advantages these might provide are likely to be extremely shortlived. Instead, true competitiveness must be built around something we all know exists but which is seldom discussed in business situations. Companies must base their temporary monopolies on emotions and imagination.

THE LAST TABOO

Exploiting the last taboo means departing from the tradition that people are to be treated as just another factor of production – a human resource or an anonymous consumer. People do not enjoy being treated as human resources or as a nameless and faceless customer x; they want to be seen and recognised as individuals. We have to tap the hidden treasures of the extended organisational tribe and its members. We have to start competing on the basis of feelings and fantasy – emotion and imagination.

Once upon a time the key materials for the creation of temporary monopolies were raw materials and hardcore technology. Today, the new raw materials are institutions, the media and perceptions.

Most individuals, consumers as well as colleagues, already are, or at least could be, driven by a rationale that extends far beyond the purely economic one. As Alberto Alessi, founder of the company with the same name, once said: 'People have an enormous need for art and poetry that industry does not yet understand.' As Alessi charges some $40 for a toilet brush, he must be doing something right.

There is money in emotion. This is not an obscure flaky agenda. It may represent the antithesis to the previous commercial rationale but it is not anti-commercialism. It is the new commercialism. It is not flaky – it is funky. Poetry and profits need not be mutually exclusive. If contemporary business was only a case of bits, brains and brands – why did Citibank work with Elton John? Why did Motorola and Microsoft team up with the Rolling Stones? And why did Miller enter an alliance with MC Hammer? And why does H&M work with Madonna? The answer is short and melodic: vibes.

Even traditional industrial firms admit that emotion and imagination are the way forward. Just listen to one of the head designers at Ford: 'In the past we tended to focus inwardly, looking for functional efficiency. Now the mindshift is to more outwardly focused, emotional satisfaction for the consumer.' It makes you wonder what old Henry would have said. Our guess would be that if it lowered costs and boosted sales, Henry would have grasped the concept immediately. Capitalists turn into humanists the instant this metamorphosis proves profitable.

The reality is that the company that aspires to be competitive cannot deprive itself of the strengths associated with what we call 'economies of soul'.

Soul is heartfelt, personal, sexual. It touches us. Not everyone wants to be touched – especially when they buy a toilet brush or a postal sorting machine. While the best (and worst) things in life are associated with strong feelings, if you mention words like love, lust, glad, wild or zany in most corporate settings, people rush from the room. Some four-letter words always offend.

Forget causing offence. IQ and EQ must coexist. In an excess economy, success comes from attracting the emotional consumer or colleague – not the rational one. But, in a day and age when you really need to know these people by heart, many executives don't even seem to know them by name.

As for our customers, economies of soul mean focusing on the extended experience, trying to look and think beyond the atoms or bits. As someone once remarked, sushi is really cold, dead fish, but that isn't what the customer buys or how it should be marketed. Then, why do so many companies still persist in selling cold, dead fish to consumers who are much more interested in sushi?

The moral: what companies sell and what their customers buy are two different things. Therefore, every once in a while it is wise to place yourself in the shoes of your customers and ask the question: What are they really buying? The answer, 99 times out of 100, is not what you think you are selling.

Economies of soul are also concerned with our colleagues. We need to

Economies of soul

understand what makes them mad, sad and glad, as Manfred Kets de Vries of Insead puts it. We need to become masters of playing the emotional strings on our own and their lyres. How can we expect to motivate and inspire people when we have not got a clue about what makes them tick? We should all learn something from Herb Kelleher at SouthWest Airlines. 'We are not afraid to talk to our people with emotions. We're not afraid to tell them, "We love you" because we do,' said Kelleher.

And profiting from soul economies begins with understanding ourselves. What really makes you mad, sad and glad? Just look at Bill Gates – his nerdship. Mr Gates created his (temporary?) monopoly by getting the Microsoft operating system into all IBM computers throughout the world. Right now, he is the richest person on Planet Earth and, together with Warren Buffett, the most generous donor through the Melinda and Bill Gates Foundation. Yet we are

The human brain is emotionally wired. The limbic system that governs our feelings always overpowers the neocortex where logic and reason rest.

sure that it is not money that drives Bill Gates. Money is merely a positive side effect.

In fact, we should all know what drives Bill because we have all met him – at least three times. The first time was in kindergarten. Bill was the tiny boy sitting outside the sandbox. Every now and then, the tough guys turned around and threw sand in his eyes. The second time was in third grade. It was gym class and time to play soccer. Bill Gates was the tiny guy, now with glasses, who got picked last – after the girls. The third time we met him was at prom night. Bill was the skinny and badly dressed guy, now with really thick glasses, standing in the corner eating snacks and drinking soda. He came alone, and none of the girls wanted to dance with him. Do you remember him now?

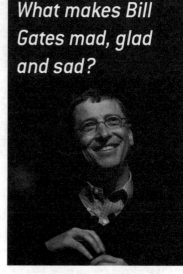

What makes Bill Gates mad, glad and sad?

What makes Bill Gates mad, sad and glad? What makes him tick? It might be – revenge. Revenge against all the kids who threw sand in his eyes, all those who neglected to pick him when it was time to play soccer, and all the girls who refused to dance with him at prom night. And if you belong to one of those groups you'd better beware, because Bill's back and this time he's in charge. Microsoft is the vehicle – revenge is the fuel. Get mad. Get even. Get happy.

INFINITE INNOVATION

Conventional levels of and perspectives on innovation will get us nowhere. Economies of soul do not emerge from predictable, incremental innovation. To be successful in the twenty-first century we will have to learn how to practise infinite innovation. Infinite innovation is the never-ending pursuit of creating more and more value for all stakeholders inside and outside the organisation. Infinite = endless. Or as Chris Bangle, head of all design at BMW, expresses it, 'It's a matter of do, do, do – Max DoDo.'

But infinite innovation also requires that we focus on the infinite aspects of what we offer prospective customers and colleagues. Infinite = limitless. Both time and space, for instance, are finite dimensions – races with finishing lines. Even if you come first, after reaching the finishing line there is nothing more to do other than hang around waiting for the competitors to arrive. Innovation may be instant and international, but it does not carry infinite opportunities. There is nothing beyond real-time and everywhere. What made Nike or Starbucks coffee-shops so successful? Well, it wasn't simply their speed or their global reach.

This does not mean that we advise organisations to go back to being slow and local. It is simply that it is hard to see how you can build *sustainable* competitive advantages in finite dimensions. What is a novelty today is bound to become a commodity next week or even tomorrow. Even worse, every time we make a move, we are also moving closer and closer to the real-time, global wall. Again, doing well in these aspects is necessary but not sufficient.

Think about when you last bought a laptop. What were the sales arguments – price, performance, weight, gigabytes and megaHertz? Well, in a true excess economy, all those are given. From a strict price/performance view it will not really matter which vacuum cleaner, TV set, DVD player or microwave the customer buys. They are all more or less equally good. Remember what JD Power said about cars, 'Today, there are no bad cars.' Getting that stuff right only buys you a ticket to take part in the game. If you and your company cannot fix the basics you are part of the crowd.

Finite dimensions also happen to be objectively measurable and clear. As a result, it is easy for consumers to evaluate the performance of different competitors. Add to this the enabling effect of the Net. Google, Yahoo and Compare Net are not only portals or search engines. They are compare engines. Finite strategies + the Net mean that comparison-shopping becomes a piece of cake for the well-informed customer. By focusing on these finite aspects of the offering, companies enable the customer to be even more demanding. Consequently, in this rational world, there is also a clear risk (or chance) that the winner will take all. Are you willing to take that bet?

Infinite dimensions, however, allow us to escape from the fate of always being at the mercy of the demanding customer. By focusing on implementing our competitive advantages in infinite dimensions, we make sure that there is no end to our endeavours. A customer offering can always become more stylish, attractive or sensational; there is no end to how friendly we can behave in relation to our customers and colleagues; there is no limit to how creative an organisation can become.

Business just isn't a finite game – never has been and never will be. Even Bill Gates admits that, 'You will never go to a Microsoft meeting and hear somebody say, "let's win" or "we won" because that has a finite scale to it.'

Moreover, infinite dimensions are open to subjective interpretations. What captures our attention may not capture yours, and vice versa. People differ in terms of what they like and dislike. Funk = diversity. Remember that for the typical masochist heaven is hell. Infinite innovation provides us with the dimensions needed to target the interests of specific tribes. Naturally, this also means saying no to certain customers. Not all people like the design of Jean-Paul Gaultier or Stella McCartney's clothes or Alessi's kettles. A lot of people genuinely disliked the Benetton ads featuring AIDS patients and pictures of war casualties from the Balkans. This was not harmful to Benetton. Indeed, it wanted a reaction. Its judgement was that its potential market would be intrigued, impressed or have different positive responses to its ads.

It is better to be something for someone rather than nothing to everyone. The danger of focusing on finite dimensions is that you may well end up as nothing to anyone.

In an emotional economy, it is better to piss off 90 per cent of the people while capturing the attention and interest of the other 10 per cent than to be merely OK to all of them. Since the early 1990s, some CDs have carried stickers with parental warnings that they contain explicit lyrics. Why not have this for all customer offerings? Explicit design Explicit content. Being banned pays. Some customers become glad, others sad or mad. But at least they feel something. They are not ignorant. Why don't we have X-rated jeans, X-rated cars or X-rated vacuum cleaners?

Be distinct in your design or be prepared to die.

This reasoning applies to all products and services in all countries. In the new world, OK, average and almost won't do. People want amazing things, spectacular things, funky things. The new economy is more like figure skating than speed skating – you score points for artistic impression (and you do need to get into the mind of the Ukrainian judge).

Sensational Strategies

To profit from infinite innovation, we need to focus our energy on a few of these more elusive dimensions. Competitive strategy is the route to nowhere. We need to create sensational strategies. Sensational strategies capture the attention of the people with whom we want to do business. Sensational strategies appeal to all five senses of man. They embrace our emotions. Competitive strategy means being one step ahead. Sensational strategy is about playing a different game.

The first sensational strategy is concerned with ethics. Today's journalists are expert at finding skeletons in our closets. In a CNN village, global gossip travels at the speed of light. Total transparency will undress the unscrupulous. People and organisations that do not understand this may find themselves removed from the hall of fame to the hall of shame. And, in this way at least, a market economy is deeply democratic. Customers vote with their money; one dollar one vote. Competents vote with their minds; one idea one vote. No capitalism without representation. If you use child labour or don't care about the environment, customers will take their business elsewhere. And so, too, will most investors and intellectuals. Few people want to work for and invest in toxic companies, as Stanford's Jeffrey Pfeffer prefers to call them. Ethics Inc. realises that one way to do well is by doing good.

All things being equal, the caring capitalist will always beat the evil enterprise. Body Shop's Anita Roddick created a temporary monopoly from the simple idea that there was a market for cosmetics that had not been tested on animals and which contained only natural ingredients. Companies increasingly want to appear caring. For example, the automotive company Toyota is not only developing hybrid technology but is currently developing trees that absorb toxic gases. Caring needs to be accompanied by credibility. Funky organisations have total ethics. Ethics must concern everyone and everything at a firm. They must be practised everywhere, continually. You just cannot be a little ethical or merely ethical when it suits you. Ethics is absolute.

In an age of affection and abundance, ethics is also a potent competitive weapon. It can provide a means of differentiation – rarely has it already been fully exploited by the competition. We can use ethics to attract new customers *and* employees. Today it's OWW4 meet PWE: Organisations Worth Working For meet People Worth Employing. As a company, you get the employees you deserve and vice versa. Do not expect anything else. From this perspective, a firm works very much like a fish. It rots from the head down. If the top of the organisation does not provide good role models, why should the rest of the organisation behave like good citizens?

The second sensational strategy focuses on aesthetics. From the global dispersion of technologies and skills it follows that most products and services are similar. So, if the interior is more or less the same, we must start competing through the exterior appearance of our products and services. Contemplate these words of wisdom from renowned designer Philippe Starck, 'People take technology for granted these days. What they want are warm, friendly products – something to seduce them.' So come on, amaze us, daze us, and seduce us – and it doesn't matter if we're talking about a TV set or an industrial compressor. Give us PWPs – Products With Personalities.

Studies suggest that for every dollar invested in design, sales rise $19. The UK Design Council developed a design index of 63 companies which use design really well. Over the past 10 years these organisations out-performed the FTSE-100 benchmark by 200 per cent.

We can see this trend towards differentiation with design throughout the business world. Companies such as Nokia and Samsung sell their mobile phones through their design. Swedish retailer H&M used to be known as a copycat in the fashion industry. Now, it has 60 in-house designers and regularly lines up with Stella McCartney, Karl Lagerfeld and Victor & Rolf for special collections that sell out within minutes. Nike goes one step further and employs 350 designers. Is your company design-driven? BMW's Chris Bangle says: 'Design is meaning.' If your company is not interested in design, it is meaningless. Everything has a form. If it has a form, it has a meaning. You have to have a design. As Chris Bangle observes, it is impossible not to have a form. But design is not only form. Design also equals functionality, costs, lifestyle and lifespan.

Design is about truth, love and beauty – and, increasingly, about whether a business has a sensational strategy or the same strategy as everyone else. In this design-driven world, everything is a fashion accessory. There is fashion in everything – the beautiful train, the aesthetic airport, the trendy wrench and the stylish lawnmower. A good price/performance relationship is necessary but no longer sufficient. Recently, one of us visited a computer games company in Silicon Valley where games are developed and launched in winter and summer collections. Fashion rules – and the only fashion victims are those who fail to keep pace. Again, this is not only a case of the limited customer offering. Aesthetics concerns all aspects of the organisation and in how we deal with customers and colleagues – the office architecture, the stores, packaging, sales people and so on.

Brands and marketing communication are part of this extended aesthetic experience. Brands that engage people emotionally can command prices that are as much as 20 to 200 per cent higher than more 'rational' competitors. In a surplus society, in which people are condemned to freedom, brands reduce uncertainty. They enable us to communicate who we are, or maybe who we would like to be. Brands implicitly convey trust and recognition. Anything can be branded. Even products that most of us never see – look at Intel. Brands make us feel safe. You are in Tokyo. Cultural mega-chock. People everywhere. Uncertainty fever. To soothe your weary head you put on your Diesel jeans, Hugo Boss shirt and Nike sneakers. You leave the W hotel and head for McDonald's to enjoy a McFeast burger and a Coke. Brands are valium for our souls – lighthouses in a chaotic world. How else can we explain the fact that 150 million Unilever products are sold every day and that 1.2 billion people daily use Gillette products? What you ask for is what you get. Zero-variance. Only foreseeable surprises. No wonder the Coca-Cola brand is worth some $70 billion. The Coca-Cola company could probably burn down all its physical assets and still go to the bank the next day to borrow a couple of million dollars. How much could you borrow? Burn it down – build something sensational.

Building the Emotional Enterprise

So, how do we unleash the potential for emotional competitiveness and corporate imagination? At least in the West, the preferred approach for handling increased organisational complexity or new organisational dimensions has been to add yet another box to the organisational chart. Somewhere in the world we are sure a manager will read this book and, as a result, set up a department for emotions and imagination. They may – to finish the job properly – appoint a male, 46.5-year-old to run the unit. Ridiculous? We hope so, but it closely resembles the way in which we have gone about handling issues such as quality and knowledge during the past 20 years. Stripping people of their freedom is not the proper response to funk.

It is ridiculous and, what's more, it doesn't work. Think of the firms that created strategic planning departments in the 1960s. Did they plan the future successfully? Did they, for example, anticipate the oil crisis of the early 1970s? Did they foresee the fall of the Berlin Wall? Professor James Brian Quinn goes as far as to say that the process of strategic planning is like a ritual rain-dance. The main objective is not to make it rain, however, but to become better dancers. Consider all the companies that set up quality departments in the 1980s. How many quality organisations can you see? There are thousands of customer service departments, yet customer service is as bad as always.

Not that long ago we did some consulting for a major department store in Sweden. The company had experienced tremendous problems with shoplifting. Finally, management decided to do something. They appointed a head of security to take care of the problem. The result: more things disappeared. The reason: by making this issue a big thing for a select few, the others stopped caring.

Message: the critical components and true sources of competitive advantage, such as knowledge, quality and people stuff, must be turned into a small thing for all people in the organisation. Funky organisations have already realised that emotion and imagination is not a department, it is a philosophy, an attitude. But they do not turn this philosophy into organisational action by merely reasoning with people – they have already moved far beyond that.

There are basically four ways in which you can communicate with people no matter who they are: you appeal to their Reason, Affection, Intuition or Desire. Whereas reason is a question of logic, affection concerns love, intuition is about second sight, and desire equals lust. Every time we communicate with someone we use a mix of R, A, I and D. Just take the latest slogan created by your organisation – a new mission statement or an ad – and rank it in terms of the four dimensions.

But the critical question is whether or not you are using a potent mix. In an age of abundance and information overload, where attention is a scarce resource, are you really getting through? Are you striking the right keys? Is something lacking? We suspect that most organisations and individuals could load their message with more feelings. Instead of just reasoning with people it is time to start AID-ing them – appealing to their affection, intuition and desire.

Most managers are experts in the first category – lawyers, engineers and MBAs alike. This is where they got their training and experience – they are playing a logic game. Reasoning is what the typical manager is rewarded for. Eventually the analytical side of the brain grows so large and heavy that some executives find it difficult to avoid walking in circles.

The problem is that in an age of affection, success depends less and less on our reasoning skills. There are millions of super-smart, IQ-packed people out there. In the new economy, it is your task to bring people on a journey into an uncertain and chaotic future – every day. As Professor Noel Tichy of the University of Michigan says, 'The best way to get people to venture into unknown terrain is to make it desirable by taking them there in their imagination.' Doing so requires that we exploit the A, the I and the D –

Reason — Head
Affection — Heart
Intuition — Gut
Desire — Groin

rather than going nowhere with rational reasoning. Stories and storytelling are about AID-ing. Spinning people does not imply more reasoning. 'You've got to evangelise the concept,' says John Chambers, chairman and CEO of Cisco Systems.

Sinnovation:
Pride
Envy
Gluttony
Lust
Anger
Greed
Sloth

The only way to create real profit is to attract the emotional rather than rational consumer and colleague by appealing to their feelings and fantasy. If you try reasoning, you will have to deal with the purely economic rationality of the demanding customer or calculating co-worker. This inevitably results in zero profits as you will compete globally with an infinite number of other similar firms. And, from an internal perspective, the best possible result is competence without commitment – the first step in performing competence castration surgery. Instead, success requires that you lower the aim from the head to the rest of the body.

The way to trick the trap of the market is to refocus from the head to the heart, gut and groin of people – to go after their affection, intuition and desire. Let's say you are throwing a party for your closest friends. What will determine whether this is to be the best party of their lives? The product: good food and a decent bottle(s) of wine will obviously help. But at least one or two of your friends could probably outperform you by turning to an even better caterer or wine store. Again the product as such is given – necessary but not sufficient. What will matter is whom you invite and how good you are at creating an attractive atmosphere.

Look at the return of music festivals. At such happenings, the audiences – the customers – are the real stars. Success and large crowds rest with turning fans into stars. Berlin is made attractive through the annual Love Parade. All cities have buildings. All cities have roads and parks. Atoms abound. It is the soft stuff that really matters. Cities also take part in the great global attraction game. And so do you. What is your organisation currently doing to make the customers feel like stars?

Involving the customers sometimes just happens. The English cricket team is now followed by a 'Barmy Army'. This collection of vocal supporters has travelled the world following the team. Cheap air travel now makes this possible for a growing number of people – when England played in the West Indies there were 10,000 English supporters; in Australia thousands more. Not content with following the team, the Barmy Army is now turning into a business, selling T-shirts and memorabilia. The followers have become the news story and a decidedly tribal business.

The same reasoning is valid in most business situations. Just look at Harley-Davidson. The company and the customer offering are not for everyone. You have to share some traits with the other members of the Harley tribe. The company is not just selling a motorcycle; it is selling American nostalgia. The arguments for buying a Harley have little to do with rational reasoning – price or performance – and everything to do with affection, intuition and desire. Says former CEO Richard Teerlink: 'There's a high degree of emotion that drives our success. We symbolise the feelings of freedom and independence that people really want in this stressful world.'

Q: 'What does Harley Davidson sell?'
A: (from HD exec.) 'The ability for a 43-year old accountant to dress in black leather, ride through small towns and have people be afraid of him.'

Or look at the Apple team that developed the first Mac. They believed their computer would change not only computing, but the whole world. The team had a soul. The members were driven by the desire to make a difference. When Steve Jobs was trying to recruit John Sculley from Pepsi, he just asked him, 'Do you want to spend the rest of your life selling sugared water, or do you want a chance to change the world?' Sculley took his chance.

It is time to start treating customers and critical competents as celebrity guests. These people show up when they want to, and they will leave when they feel like it. To keep them happy, we can't just sit back and do nothing. There is no way we can talk them into staying. We have got to prove our commitment in action by entertaining them – keeping them happy. We have to create *emotional switching costs*. Building a true tribe means instituting the same kind of relationships that (used to?) exist in a family. Breakups, divorces and unexpected deaths or lost customers and defecting

Break-ups should result in anxiety

employees should result in a lot of anxiety – on both sides.

If you think this sounds excessive then listen to Ken Alvares, speaking when he led worldwide human resources at Sun Microsystems. He said that the goal 'is to keep people so busy having fun every day that they don't even listen when the headhunters call'. We all know that happy people do a better job, but how many companies have words such as fun and happiness included in their vision or mission statements? Remember that a pretty good predictor of a company's performance is the average number of laughs per employee per day.

The Average Never Ever Wins

In an age of affection, all organisations compete with each other. The industries, regions and markets they are active in no longer really matter. Competition is not specific and centred on providing great jobs or products, excellent services or career opportunities. In the emotional economy, competition is generic and revolves around who can provide people, consumers and co-workers with a good life. It is about providing people with dreams. And the definition of what this life really means will differ from tribe to tribe, person to person, and from time to time. The important thing is that we are in charge.

There is no doubt that we are going to see tremendous wealth creation in the years to come. The trillion-dollar question is: who is going to share this wealth? Of one thing we can be sure: the average never wins. It never has and never will. What is different in the age of abundance is that the average is currently getting an additional three billion new individual members, an uncountable number of new companies and a plethora of new products and services. Even so, looking forward 10 years, your greatest competitors are probably still unborn and unknown. And all these individuals and organisations want to share the new wealth – they want a piece of the cake.

To succeed, we must stop being so goddamn normal. If we behave like all the others, we will see the same things, come up with similar ideas and develop identical products or services. At its best, normal output will produce normal results. In a winner takes all world, normal = nothing. But if we are willing to take one little risk, break one tiny rule, disregard a few of the norms, there is at least a theoretical chance that we will come up with something different, actually get a niche, create a short-term monopoly and make a little money.

Funky business is like playing the lottery. If you participate, there is a 99 per cent chance that you will lose. On the other hand, if you do not take part, your chances of losing are 100 per cent. To succeed we have to go for that single per cent. The future belongs to the outliers – those who dare to take risks, break rules and make new ones. The future belongs to those who seize the opportunity to create it.

So, if we are indeed living in a surplus society, an emotional economy, on the verge of friction-free capitalism, what can we do? Well, the answer is quite simple. Our only chance of surviving and thriving in this crazy world is to excel in exploiting the last taboo.

People expect good stuff. They have become used to great value for money. And

People and organisations of the world – come out

they can get that from almost all companies around the world. So, being great is no longer good enough. Customer satisfaction is not enough. To succeed we have to surprise people. We have to attract and addict them. Attraction and attention is all. By focusing only on the hardcore aspects of business we risk becoming irrelevant. And trust us, irrelevancy is a much greater problem that inefficiency. The only thing more difficult than learning to exploit the last taboo of emotion and imagination is learning to thrive without it. So, people and organisations of the world – come out. Or you will be carried out

PHOTO CREDITS